Family as
Primary Educator

A SOCIOLOGICAL STUDY

Family as Primary Educator

A SOCIOLOGICAL STUDY

AURORA BERNAL

FRANCISCO ALTAREJOS

ALFREDO RODRÍGUEZ

Scepter

Contents

Foreword

The university is and should be an appropriate place to seek and find truth. Sincere dialogue and group effort are required; this endeavor is a service to persons and to society. Recognizing this challenge, the Institute of Family Sciences at the University of Navarra has devoted itself to scientific research on marriage and the family and the task of forming specialists at an advanced level. The present book reflects this effort.

Ours is an age in which new ideas and new realities clash and compete with the old ones. In this time of general confusion, the authors present a "clarifying" image of the family. Two realities must be kept in mind. First, as is demonstrated here, the family is prior to society. It is important to avoid the reductionism often found in family studies drawn from an exclusively sociological analysis. Second, the family is the foundation of personal relationships and the place where all the possible social relationships are tried out. The family is not just the basic cell of society—a subject on which a surprising consensus is now emerging. It is the place where every human being has his origin and personal development begins. The authors of the present volume see the family as a perfect institution (because it includes all the ends of the person) but also an insufficient one (because it does not have all the means to attain those goals).

The first chapter, "Changes and expectations in the family," by professor Francisco Altarejos, brings us quickly to the heart of the matter: "The current crisis of the family consists of the inadequacy of today's understanding of the *traditional family*." Not all elements that constitute the traditional family are disposable; many retain their validity, because they are constituent elements of a permanent familial reality that can be called the *original family*. The task at hand is to delve deeper into those constituent elements in order to grasp their relevance to new situations. The mission of the family as an *original community of persons*, consists in the actualization and fulfillment of its original nature through its members' growth. The family affirms and perfects its members through its care for life as a community.

Fully understanding this reality requires the use of an interdisciplinary lens. Thus the chapters that follow pursue the subjects from the viewpoints of sociology, anthropology, philosophy, and educational theory.

Operating from an anthropological perspective in the second chapter, Francisco Altarejos, Alfredo Rodríguez, and Aurora Bernal show that the family is the natural environment for the development of the deep human tendency not only to live but to live with others. In discovering the possibilities of this coexistence, one understands that the family is also an environment where each person finds his identity and discloses it through his relationship with those close to him. The family provides the experience of diversity through life with other members of the family. "Intimacy heightens the intensity of these relationships." Sociability expands and takes shape as *coexistence as a way of life*.

In the third chapter, Alfredo Rodríguez considers a subject often debated. The title sums it up: "'Families' and the family." The methodology, taken from Weber, focuses on *social types*. Avoiding the reductionism, however, professor Rodríguez states: "The question, then, is not to defend or affirm the traditional family as preferable, better, or truer, but to show that the original family cannot be reduced to just one more social type of any possible kind." In the fourth chapter, Aurora Bernal examines the educational value of interpersonal relationships established in the family. She emphasizes that the family is "an anthropological reality—relational—required by the constitution of the human being—also a relational being." It follows that the interpersonal relationships that constitute the reality of the family express the *dialogical* nature of the human being. Family relationships are worthy of respect; but not all possible forms of relationship are equally educational, and we can distinguish which empower persons and which do not. The relationships established by maternity, paternity, filiation, and fraternity are humanizing and personalizing. The author provides an anthropological account of the family as the place where one learns to handle one's freedom, be who one is, and form a community out of society.

"Confidence and respect" are the key notions in the fifth chapter. Professor Concepción Naval shows how these values are developed in the family environment. Confidence or trust is a radical element of human encounters. "It is the relational source of human love, which is the root of the security that the person needs, and particularly the child. It is the seedbed of the feelings of security, which are irreplaceable when one deals with the frequent edges and roughness of social relationships." By means of confidence, other tendencies such as generosity and altruism, emerge and become consolidated as positive habits of human relationships until they flower as social or public virtues like affability and truthfulness. Those habits, which originate within the family, are often missing in contemporary social life.

In the sixth chapter, finally, Gerardo Castillo explains one of the most basic elements of education within the family: education in freedom and affectivity. This is a perennial subject: "As freedom, more than a quality to be expanded, is a task to be realized, the family is the original environment for the consolidation and growth of freedom, which will be realized later in other fields, including professional work, social relationships, and even *leisure time.*" Freedom requires overcoming domination by feelings.

Once again the necessary role of the family is shown. The development of human powers arising from intimacy takes place in family life. Professor Castillo describes what is most significant with reference to freedom and affections in the different stages of personal growth.

No single book or research project says all there is to say about the family. Here is one of the greatest contributions of this book: It opens the door to numerous additional questions that need answers, while providing a helpful framework. One of these questions, of primary importance, concerns the community character of the family. It in turn will point the way to the family in its original sense.

I sincerely thank the authors for their efforts and for their valuable cooperation in the research projects of the Institute of Family Sciences. Works of this depth guarantee a promising future and contribute to a more humane and united society.

Javier Escrivá-Ivars
Pamplona, March 2005

CHAPTER 1

CHANGES AND EXPECTATIONS IN THE FAMILY

(Francisco Altarejos)

1. TODAY'S FAMILY CRISIS

What is a family? That question would have received a quick and easy answer years ago. Today few would ask it expecting to get a simple response. The problem often is said to stem from profound changes affecting family life in recent decades. From a sociological perspective, one can also agree with A. Giddens: "Of all the changes happening in the world, none is more important than the ones taking place in our private life, in sexuality, relationships, marriage, and the family. A worldwide revolution is going on, about how we consider ourselves, and how we develop bonds and relationships with others."[1]

In answering the question, this process of transformation can itself serve as a point of departure. The notion of "change" is not precise, but instead has various significant aspects. For example, to change does not always imply discarding what is being changed. "Transformation" comes closer to the mark, for in signifying a change in form, it implies permanence in what is

---

1. A. Giddens, *Un mundo desbocado. Los efectos de la globalización en nuestras vidas* (Madrid: Taurus, 2000): 65.

1

being transformed along with some modification. Despite the haste to issue a death certificate for the patriarchal or traditional family—something today undeniable in the West—it may not be dead but may be undergoing reform or alteration, positive or negative depending on what actually is done.

The structure of the traditional family no doubt has suffered radical modifications due to the impact of factors arising from the "open" or "complex" society. These include: the absorption of the woman into the working world and her distancing from domestic work; the decline of the principle of authority, which breaks down the cohesion of family life; increased migration, which undermines a stable home environment; cultural change leading to ethical relativism; the explosion of consumerism upon the family economy; the mass media; and so on. There are countless ways to explain the decisive transformation of the family during the twentieth century. All have their own validity and explanatory power.

Nevertheless, the multiple explanations share a common failing: all are merely explanations. We think we know what is happening, but there is more that needs explaining. The radical question, put crudely, is: "Now what?" It has no clear answer, perhaps because there are so many different, contradictory answers—so many proposals regarding what can be done that in the end no one really is sure about what to do. More than simple ignorance, this uncertainty may reflect a fear of commitment, since that would require a simple answer to a simple question: what is the family?

With all these uncertainties and hesitancies, however, there is at least one undeniable certainty, at least as long as the United Nations' Universal Declaration of Human Rights remains in effect. This is the central and radical character of family life in society, as expressed in article 15: "The family is the natural and fundamental element of society, and it is entitled to protection by the society and the State." Obviously, this is not insight achieved at some particular time and place. Rather it is the acknowledgment in a concrete historical moment—in Paris, December 10, 1948, by Resolution No 217/III—of a fact that is not subject to historical conditioning. Not every human being comes into the world as part of a family, but all need to *become humanized* in one. The objections raised for several decades now by persons citing primitive cultures in which the clan or tribe minimized or replaced the family in the formation of its society, not only are atypical but turn out to be irrelevant from a statistical, scientific, and commonsensical point of view, even though at times they are presented with the pretension of being scientific contributions that explain the most important of all human phenomena. But the data are few in number, more picturesque than relevant, and more extravagant than significant; taken together, they do not provide definitive answers but only exotic hypotheses. Far from providing certitude, the results of such research end in a kind of cultural relativism, leading to generalized uncertainty or, in the best case, a questionable interpretation about which even the authors argue.[2]

Not only in the West, but also in the East—and especially vigorously there—the family is experienced as the "natural and fundamental element of society" as proclaimed by the Universal Declaration of Human Rights. As an old expression puts it, the family universally appears as the *basic cell* of society. This solidly rational and vital certainty, however, does not now point to any further, comparable certainties. On the contrary, doubts abound when, as often happens today, the question is, "What family are we talking about?" The family is a principle of great importance and vital interest; yet accepting it as a natural and fundamental element of society appears to be intellectually beyond the pale.

---

2. R. Parkin, L. Stone, eds., *Kinship and Family: An Anthropological Reader* (Boston: Blackwell, 2004).

This loss of fundamental certainty suggests that the doubts and suspicions are not grounded in the reality of the family but in concepts, consciousness, and knowledge influenced by the epistemological requirements of a method of research. The problem does not concern the present situation of the family but the way it presently is understood—or, more correctly, with contemporary ignorance about the reality of the family. This is due mainly to the fact that the family's existence as a stable, permanent social structure contradicts today's common suppositions about the nature of society itself, preferentially understood (according to the distinction of F. Tönnies) as an *association*[3]— that is, a human group that:

a) is established with determined and concrete goals, that have been freely set;

b) has a contractual, legal character; and

c) is developed by the *mechanical* working of intersubjective relationships.

At the basis of all proposed "new models" of the family we find this basic form of *association*—a group constituted to serve the voluntary objectives or goals that its members choose. Recent pressures for legalization—that is, social acceptance and recognition—of other forms of private groupings, such as "common law couples" or homosexual unions, have as their real intentions, first, to demand the same rights for natural children as for legitimate ones and, second, to be able to adopt children, whom they cannot naturally beget.

In the drive for legalization and social recognition of such personal unions one nevertheless can discern a desire on the part of those pressing such goals to constitute themselves as a family; and this clearly shows the family's universal value. The

3. F. Tönnies, *Community and Association* (C. P. Loomis, translator) (London: Routledge & Kegan Paul, 1974).

most ardent advocates are those who most strongly desire the status of being married. That these stable couples—so called for want of an adjective that suits their particular shared lives—attempt to equate their union to marriage, including all of its rights, and desire to incorporate children as sons and daughters into their everyday lives, demonstrates that the family based on marriage is universally recognized as a *natural and fundamental* element.

The question of the family is intricate and complex, now and always, but its diagnosis is not. The "crisis of the traditional family" does not seem to affect its persistence, as demonstrated by those who propose to change the model of family while trying to preserve its intrinsic value. As was foreseeable, this attempt to change the model gives rise to a disconcerting diversity of models. If the family is an association in the sense described above, this result is inevitable, due to the proliferation of subjective goals, voluntary ends, and personal situations.

In this way the unique, unequivocal meaning of family is replaced by an equivocal one. Social confusion results, making necessary a resort to a mechanism that will convert diversity into homogeneity. Marriage and family then are reduced to a specific form of legal contract. The primary goal is to regulate personal relationships, establishing rights and duties of family members among themselves and, above all, toward society in general. But human relationships treated primarily from the perspective of legal regulations will have a positivistic, artificial character by contrast with genuinely personal relationships, which are fluid and natural. The fundamental difference lies in the difference between two essential forms of human relationship: association and *community*.

Originally, the family is understood more as a community than an association—in other words, as a unit of shared life in which:

a) the ends are the persons involved;

b) the legal contract defines the commitment only partially, since the family is based on a personal commitment of an ethical character; and

c) growth takes place through free acts of interpersonal
accepting and self-giving.

"Community" is defined as the quality of commonality,
which, not being private, pertains or extends to various people.
To say it is not private indicates that participation involves a
sharing without anyone's diminishment.[4] The acts themselves
of community members are acts of communion, generically
defined as "participation in the common" and more specifically,
as communication among people. Hence the definition of family offered by John Paul II:[5] "a community of persons" (*com-
munio personarum*), a meaning with anthropological resonance
by which the author roots the crucial mission of the family as
the "most complete and richest school of humanity." This is a
conception of family not usually taken seriously in family-
related research.

2. SOCIOLOGICAL ASPECTS

Present-day confusions about the family have more to do with
current understandings for "family" than with real-life problems. This is to say that the problems are theoretical. It is true
that difficulties and problems have always existed in families.
There are happy families, but none without problems. In this
sense, Tolstoy's well-known statement in *Anna Karenina*—
"All happy families are alike; each unhappy family is unhappy in
their own way"—is not true. The opposite seems to be the case.

---

4. The root of the word "community" has the same meaning as in communication
where both parties share something fully with no loss to either.

5. John Paul II, *Familiaris Consortio*, No. 21, (2000).

Unhappy families have recurring problems: alcohol, gambling, infidelity, lack of involvement with the children. But there are many different situations in happy families: in sickness or in health, for richer or for poorer, the emptiness of death, and so on. Tolstoy's vision is limited to external appearances. The present crisis of the family is undeniable, but this crisis concerns the *traditional family*. In speaking superficially of the traditional family, one is speaking of a structure of coexistence, recognized by the law and society, with economic and educational consequences. The focus is on formal elements—a legal contract between a man and a woman, unity of life, children to come, a division of labor (for men usually outside the home, for women usually within it). Or else the family is viewed as an intergenerational compact, with adults providing for the education of the young.[6]

But structures do not exhaust the reality of the family. People are not *only* "children of their times," but they do live in a historical context. Long-lasting realities, therefore, have a special significance, and the family is one. A person must confront the problems of his times, confident that, in the end, the challenge will lead him to deeper understanding and increased self-giving and humanization—of the world and also of himself.

The present crisis of the family resides in too little understanding of the traditional family. It does not follow, however, that all elements of the traditional family can therefore be discarded. Many are and will remain fully valid, because they correspond to a temporal reality that we may call the *original family*. There is a difference between overcoming and transcending. Overcoming means discarding that which is overcome. Transcending means keeping, modifying, and improving it. This is the fundamental task of any study that attempts to benefit the family. What is in question is not just a blind defense

---

6. J. Elzo, et al., *Hijos y padres. Comunicación y conflictos* (Madrid: FAD, 2002).

of the old values and structures of the traditional family, but improving them, adjusting them to present conditions. For example: authority is exercised differently now than it was in the past; but the rise of democracy does not bring about a "democratic family" or the abandonment of authority.

The United Nations declared 1994 an International Year of the Family. In the forty-six years since the Declaration of Human Rights the understanding of the family had changed. Certainty that the family was the natural and fundamental element of society had grown weaker, though it had not been abandoned. Recent documents of the UN seem to have a different perspective on the family. From the concept of *basic cell* came "the right to protection by the society and the government," implying for them a character subsidiary to the family. This change in the perception of the family can be seen in the proposal in 2004, on the tenth anniversary of the International Year of the Family, of six lines of research:

a) Fundamental criteria for family policies

b) Relative indicators of family well-being

c) HIV/AIDS and its consequence for the family

d) Retirement and its impact on the family

e) Family enterprises and economic development

f) Social functions in the spheres of socialization and aid to families.[7]

These research objectives reflect an analysis of the structural and situational changes pertaining to the family, under these five headings:

a) Changes of family structure

b) The increase of migration

---

7. Cf. U.N. General Assembly, *Preparation for the Tenth Anniversary of the International Year of the Family in 2004.* *07-17-2002, Resolution A/57/139, No. 9.

c) Demographic aging

d) The HIV/AIDS pandemic

e) The effects of globalization on the family.

The last in particular impedes basic family functions, according to the UN. The conclusion is that these trends "impose a heavy burden on family members, affecting their capacity to fulfill their basic functions of production, reproduction, and socialization."[8] The vision of reality has changed. The family is no longer the natural and fundamental cell of society, and it is now necessary instead to "reevaluate the social function of the family."[9] Society and government should still protect the family, but the emphasis is different. The family is no longer a reality prior to society, but an element at its service. Promoting the family means solving problems that disturb the social function. Although humanitarian purposes underlie this respectable position, it is debatable as a basis for determining real family needs.

The social tendencies mentioned above are real, and affect the family in a negative way. If promoting the family is subordinated to such tendencies as these and to social phenomena, however, their priority would shape the new social function of the family, according to these documents of the UN. This is not to deny the social function of the family, but neither should the family be defined by social function. This subtle difference has to be taken into account. For example, the National Statistical Institute states: "The family is universally recognized as an engine of economic development, so its needs must be considered in policy setting."[10] In this way, efforts to favor the family

---

8. Ibid., No 13.

9. A. Bernal, "*Hace diez años: Año Internacional de la Familia,*" *Estudios sobre Educación* (6), (Pamplona, 2004): 78.

10. I.N.E., *Cifras,* May 15, 2004; *http://www.ine.es/revistas/cifine_15mayo.pdf.*

often assign precedence to social benefits, with the understanding of the family reduced to its social contribution.

In summary, the change in our understanding of the family in recent decades is as important as today's family crisis itself. The present tendency is to consider the family from the point of view of its social functions, as stated in the UN document: production, reproduction, socialization. These functions are real, but they are only consequences of the family's true nature. We are witnessing the confusion of cause with effect and need to consider the family *from the inside*. Prior to its social functions comes what has always been the family's main role: the *upbringing of children*. This mission uncovers a covenant existing among family members from which the social functions emerge.

It is true that the family is a productive, reproductive, and socializing unit, but these valuable social elements come from the affirmation, development, and enhancement of the family community. Parents must help their children grow as persons, so that in due course they will also become productive, will reproduce, and will socialize (themselves and others). This process is called *education*; it is an essential mission of the family. We lose sight of this in directing attention to society's needs, no matter how important they may be. As a result, "education in the family continues to be ignored in the proposals of the United Nations as well as in some centers of research of great prestige . . . . What is urgent ultimately displaces what is important."[11]

The sociological perspective must be transcended in order to reach the ultimate reality of the family. Sociological analysis undoubtedly is valuable, but to give it the last word in questions of understanding and judgment is a surrender to *sociologism*, which is unscientific and an ideological affectation that uses sociology for its own ends, especially control. Sociologism

---

11. A. Bernal, "*Hace diez años,*" 86.

is a variant of scientism, defined in the dictionary of the Royal Academy of the Spanish language as:

a) A theory according to which things may be known as they are in reality through science, and scientific research is sufficient to satisfy the needs of human intelligence;

b) A theory according to which scientific methods must embrace the whole of the intellectual and moral life;

c) A theory according to which the valid knowledge is acquired only through positive sciences, and the mind has no other role beyond entering into these disciplines;

d) Full confidence in the principles and results of scientific research, and strict practice of its methods;

e) The tendency to give excessive value to scientific notions or notions alleged to be scientific.

This idea of "notions alleged to be scientific" is essential to understanding not only scientism but the exclusion of any way of knowing reality not based on scientific method, so that other kinds of knowledge do not even deserve criticism but are rejected outright as useless.

All the same, scientism is a degenerate by-product of scientific research. True science recognizes that it has a valuable but restricted role in acquiring knowledge of reality. Scientism is an abuse of science, used to satisfy suspect interests in the quest for solutions to real problems.

To identify family functions as related to production, reproduction, and socialization is a kind of sociological reductionism, which exhibits the "fallacy of simplification"[12] in judgments that at best are only descriptive and are statements not of fact, but of probability. Such reductionism is as familiar to the scientist as to the peasant, who draws inferences from his experience.

---

12. Cf. E. Morin, *Introducción al pensamiento complejo* (Barcelona: Gedisa, 1997): 96.

Data become meaningful only when they are integrated by an intellect; otherwise they are just a mass of data.

These principles are not intrinsic to the positive sciences; they require a superior knowledge, capable of unifying and conferring meaning on isolated facts. One often hears "it is a fact that . . . " stated as a final argument. From a logical point of view, however, the statement is not conclusive, nor does it explain anything. On the contrary, facts require explanations to be fully understood, and explanations do not come from mere statements of facts.

Our understanding of the family must conform to the descriptive sciences, but that is not the sum total of it; other principles, not found in the positive sciences, must be considered as well. These principles are as rigorous and true as those of positive science. Such knowledge is not esoteric, not a species of Gnosticism; it is true knowledge, though presently overlooked. Its sources are anthropological and philosophical ethics.

3. ETHICAL AND ANTHROPOLOGICAL CONSIDERATIONS

Anthropology and ethics, free from the limitations of empiricism and positivism, can offer a synthesis based not on an accumulation of data but on the integral consideration of reality. They do not contradict the positive human sciences, but complement them. This can be seen in some passages of the apostolic exhortation *Familiaris Consortio* by John Paul II, published in 1981. Four general tasks for the family are identified here.

1) Forming a community of persons.
2) Serving life.
3) Participating in the development of society.
4) Sharing in the life and mission of the Church.[13]

---

13. John Paul II, *Familiaris Consortio*, No. 17.

What is involved here is not described in terms of functions but of commitments, with a significant ethical content. The point is not the superiority of commitment to function; it is that there is an essential difference between the two. A commitment can be revoked but not revised, as a function can be. From a comparison between *Familiaris Consortio* and the UN statement we find the following relationships:

a) Production and reproduction are included in service to life.

b) Socialization derives from participation in the development of society.

c) The mission of the family involves other functions like assisting and caring for life and practicing solidarity through participation in society.

d) A specifically religious task is mentioned in the fourth item on the list. Evidently, then, the unifying principle here is not religious but anthropological and ethical.

e) "Forming a community of persons," provides a rationale for the other three tasks from the anthropological and ethical points of view.

As we saw above, *raising children* has traditionally been understood as the essential mission of the family. This has not been changed by the new models of family. The desire that a family be a *community* can be seen in demands to legitimize adoption and child-rearing for the sake of forming a community of persons.

Raising children is a proper and radical mission for all the forms of family. It is a common experience that educating children leads to the ongoing continuous education of parents, not only through the study of new methods but through the joint activity and the very practice of family life. Raising children is accomplished in the formation of a community of persons.

4. THE FAMILY AS A COMMUNITY OF PERSONS

To speak of the family as an educational environment is another way of expressing its primary and radical mission, namely, the formation of a community of persons, considered from the anthropological and ethical perspective. Note that the *community* in question is one of persons. The person is fundamental in the consideration of the original family.

E. Morin points to a tendency to overlook a fundamental element in analyzing the complexity of organizations made up of human beings: beyond the difference or singularity of individuals, "each individual is a subject."[14] To consider the human being as a *subject* is a first, abstract approximation of the concept of person, that conveys added meaning with respect to human organizations. This is a reminder that the person does not tolerate being considered an *object*. This is another expression of the well-known ethical principle of Kant that one should always treat a human being—oneself and other persons alike—as an end and never as a means.[15] To be treated as an object is unpleasant for a human being, because man goes far beyond such a category, which tends to be used in generic statements, such as "man is like . . . ", or "man is a being who . . . "

Although every human person participates in humankind, each one is concrete and singular. His behavior is an answer to the question *who am I?*—an answer with considerable depth. By comparison, the answer to *what am I?* will only be partial. To consider him a subject is insufficient, except in logical and semantic contexts, and results in the "most mysterious and elusive" reality.[16] From the idea of humanity, which is

---

14. E. Morin, *Introducción al pensamiento*, 96.

15. I. Kant, *Fundamentación de la metafísica de las costumbres*, 2th sección, 429, 10 (Barcelona: Ariel, 1996): 189.

16. J. Marías, *Mapa del mundo personal* (Madrid: Alianza Editorial 1994): 9.

a generalization, the person appears as an *individual*, a particular element of the group.

Man, as an individual, can be seen in different ways depending on what group one considers. People belong to different groups and classes, and may be considered objectively in different lights, depending on the group or class involved. In the political order, a man can be defined by nationality; in the social order, by customs; in the cultural order, by language; and in the ethical order, by virtues: generosity, laboriousness, justice, bravery, etc. All this tells us *what* a man is. But from a radical anthropological point of view, a man resists being considered simply as an individual, because each person is unique—not just *what* but *who*, not something but someone. This anthropological perspective is natural within the family, where the members are not valued for *what* they are, but are loved for *who* they are: or, more precisely, loved simply because they exist.

In summary, the human being, generically an individual, is a person. Individual and person are complementary, not contradictory, although conflict can arise if the human being is reduced to an individual and not a person. In many human organizations, particularly those engaged in production, people are rightly considered as individuals, inasmuch as what is being considered as their function in relation to the objectives of the organization. This is true of associations with specific and concrete goals. Yet the personal nature of the members may be taken into consideration, although not necessarily *as* members of the association.

Thus, associations are not necessarily depersonalizing. On the contrary, when the personhood of individuals is considered, an association can become a community. "Individual" and "person" are not opposites that exclude each other, and by the same token associations and communities do not exclude each other either. Indeed, one never finds pure associations or communities. There is something unnatural about consistently

ignoring human personhood; as has happened historically in
dehumanized groups in which individuals are regarded simply
as interchangeable, functional elements. This has happened in
authoritarian contexts, where social goals have a kind of
sacred aura, as well as in some revolutionary or even commer-
cial settings.

Within every community are functions that must be carried
out. Demanded by the dynamic of human life, these require a
division of labor. No community of human persons, one might
say, is purely that, nor are the persons in any community certain
of being treated always and only as persons. A mother may be
considered as a domestic worker, a father as a source of income,
children as elements to satisfy the emotional needs of parents.
In all these cases, the family is at risk of becoming a private association whose members are easily replaceable individuals. The
family, then, is not a pure and absolute community; yet it was
that *originally*, because it is founded on love. As an *original
community of persons*, then, the family's mission is to actualize
and perfect its original nature. This means the growth of its life
as a community through the growth of its members as persons

It is in this way that the reality of the family can be seen as
that of an educational environment. "The idea of environment
is part of its essential meaning."[17] The educational aspect adds
another dimension. Among the meanings of environment is:
"an ideal space involving several related activities or disciplines."* This is relevant to our study in several ways.

a) An environment can be immaterial with its existence in
    time rather than space. The notion of *home* is multidi-
    mensional, involving both place and feelings. This is
    clear in the case of geographically dispersed families. If
    the authentic character of a family exists, geographical

---

17. E. Martín López, *Familia y sociedad. Una introducción a la sociología de la familia*
(Madrid: Rialp, 2000): 46.

dispersion is unimportant, as is apparent at family reunions. Even where the affective tone of a particular family is negative, it is open to improvement.

b) Environment has limits, but these also can be immaterial as well as physical. In the case of the family, the environment extends as far as intimacy does. The environment, then, is an "*interior space* where persons relate and an exterior one consisting of relationships and social actions."[18]

The environment is shaped by the actions of the family members. These actions cannot be considered in isolation, however. They are always *interactions* between persons. This is important for the study of the family and decisive for promoting family coexistence. When actions are looked at in isolation, they give rise to true and legitimate political, sociological, psychological, and even ethical statements. But these statements do not exhaust the reality of the family and its interactions. Only *with others* does one become oneself in a family.

Individualism is the cancer of family coexistence. The ordinary term for this in Spain is liberal individualism. It is a problem for family cohesion because of the egotistical ethos to which it gives rise unless relationships are raised to the level of personal coexistence within an environment of persons living together.

Personhood that transcends mere individuality is not an option to be rejected at will. It is essential to the reality of the family and the key to its excellence as a human community, above every other society or association. Here is the basis for recognizing the dignity of the human person. A human person is an unrepeatable reality. Every human being shares human nature, and this defines what he is; but *who* he is—in other words, that he *is*, that he exists—goes beyond this. Human dignity does not reside only with humankind; it resides with

18. Ibid.

each individual who is a person. If dignity were a property of humanity in general, it would be acceptable to eliminate some individuals for the benefit of the rest. The number of individuals involved would not affect its value of dignity in that case. But human dignity is naturally and irrevocable affirmed of the human person, not realized by proclamations or speeches but in the daily life of the family; it requires protection and promotion of the family by society and the government. It would make no sense for society to ignore its original source, the family community.

Human dignity is lived naturally in the family, a community whose end is the perfecting of the persons that compose it. An essential part of human dignity is this growth of persons. An essential aspect of family reality is promoting the bodily and spiritual development of the persons who compose it. It follows that to recognize the mission of the family as forming a community of persons is equivalent to defining the family as *a community for the formation of persons*.

5. EDUCATIONAL ASPECTS

Although education in the family has been studied extensively, not so much research has been done on how the family itself is educational. The rest of this book deals with this aspect of the family and examines the formation of persons and the demands of the original family, the community of persons.

5.1. Social types and singular persons

In the nineteenth century, via the positivism of Comte, "social" became the fundamental category for understanding man. According to Comte, all other questions derive their meaning from the social perspective.

This anthropological primacy of the social is stressed by Durkheim, who proposed to establish the hegemony of the supreme human science, sociology. This marks the arrival of sociologism whose tenets were:

a) Science is a legitimate replacement for religion.

b) Religion is no more than a social institution.

c) All human action is reduced to social action.

This sociologism has three postulates that form the human sciences and define our knowledge of man.

a) Social facts are realities *sui generis*, different from individual reality, illuminated by and through the collective conscience considered as the determinative guide of human action. Individual conscience is a mere spark of this collective conscience.

b) In the relationship between individual and society, society has primacy. The idea of the individual originates here and here is most fully expressed.

c) Social facts are not explained by individual actions but by the dynamic of the social causes. This gives rise to ethical relativism, which Durkheim attempts to counter through a vigorous affirmation of social morality, that is, society as the supreme source of morality.

There is no empirical demonstration of these postulates, yet Durkheim announces them as absolute principles for understanding human reality and the explanation of individual behavior. The actions of individuals are always, by definition, social actions, in the sense that they are only understood with reference to the collective conscience. Morality is completely social and has a conventional character—"constructive" in modern terminology. Interpreting social phenomena by the collective conscience, individuals establish the rules of the game that will guide the coexistence and development of society.

The next step in this agenda is the establishment of social types, realized by Weber. These are ideal models that explain social phenomena which occur frequently and also lay the foundation for them. In Weber's analysis, the types can justify what they explain, as is done in the ethical theory of values that justify and give meaning to moral action. This is a position deeply rooted in modern sensibilities: it is not so important to know what things are, but what they mean for me, and my interests.

In this way, ideal types seem to help in our understanding of social phenomena. But, being generalizations, they block our knowledge of singular realities. The human being, as a social agent, operates according to his participation in a given social type that explains and justifies him. There are no singular actions by particular individuals; everything is a consequence of the values embodied in the types.

In this framework of man as a social agent, the family is no more than a minute social group which can respond to diverse social types. Here is the origin of the current understanding of the question of "diverse models of family," all of them legitimate and acceptable alternatives in the eyes of society and law. The traditional or patriarchal family is one more among others; its pretensions to absolute validity are unacceptable from the political, legal, or social perspectives thought to be scientifically illegitimate.

The point is not to defend the traditional family as preferable, better, or truer. It is that the original family cannot be reduced to a social type of this or that kind. Here the notion of environment becomes meaningful, since the family is an environment in which different individual types live and act. The family environment provides a framework for the growth and human development of its members. Each family has its own character, similar to but also different from that of others.

This is a deep and luminous idea: The formation of a community of persons is not realized through the medium of social types but through the joint and complementary expansion of the personalities of family members and the interactive development of habits. Each person brings his or her personal ingredient to the family environment and adopts the tone of the shared mores and family habits. Family education is precisely the joint and cooperative formation of ethically good habits.

5.2. *Identity and family coexistence*

This formation of habits in the family does not take place through instructional programs or planned moral teaching. In the family environment, shared actions are more important than words; education does not take place through objective communication but through communication that is subjective or existential (Gabriel Marcel, Karl Jaspers, Max Scheler). Teaching takes place within the family, but not as it does in a formal school. The teaching consists of the example of personal action in the daily life of each member, not stated but *demonstrated*. "Education is the product of being more than knowing; one teaches by being more than by talking" (Rassam). One might say that *co-existential praxis* is the ideal or proper form of family education.

For this co-existential praxis every element of family life is important and has educational character. For example, the basic function of feeding and providing material care for children becomes a form of primary education about welfare—not only education for wellness but especially for a good life. In this way the family can educate positively about consumerism, not by its rejection or denial, but by inculcating positive attitudes embedded in individual behavior.

In this way, too, sociability is taught, but not through lectures about its importance. The teaching consists of developing natural tendencies. Sociability, as one of these, is defined as "characteristics of one who is naturally inclined towards social behavior." It is the manifestation of something radical to the person: *coexistence*. Man, in a proper sense, does not simply exist but coexists.[19] And the family is the natural habitat for the development of this profound human tendency. This appears from recent studies dealing with social policies that concern the family community.

Practical politics confirms a decrease in social participation that is blamed on exaggerated individualism harmful to public life. More than just a recurring social problem, this is a perversion of a natural tendency to life with others expressed in sociability. Indeed, individualism is the methodological focus of much current research dealing with individuality and its psychosocial processes. Critics propose a remedy based on the family as community, and its influence on the wider society.[20]

Family education also is relevant to the question of identity. The crisis of personal identity goes hand in hand with the crisis of social participation. As the individual subject finds himself without any bonds, identity must be "constructed" autonomously—in relation to others, obviously, but not in dependence on them. Here was a recurring issue in the polemic between neo-liberals and communitarians in the 1990s: the decisive role of family roots, leading to continuity of social participation. Concern for identity and sociability, frequently associated with socialization, remains an important element in debates on political theory, especially among those concerned about anthropological and ethical issues. It has even been called "the greatest challenge at the end of [last] century"[21]—a challenge involving society and the person and aspiring to an integration of identity that at the same time respects the diversity of its elements. The problem can relate to both national and

---

19. L. Polo, *Antropología Trascendental I* (Pamplona: EUNSA, 1999): 32–33.

20. K. Bogenschneider, "Has Family Policy Come of Age? A Decade Review of the State of U.S. Family Policy in the 1990s," in R. M. Milardo, ed., *Understanding Families. Into the New Millenium: A Decade in Review* (Lawrence: NCFR, 2001): 358.

21. C. Naval, *Educar ciudadanos* (Pamplona: EUNSA, 1995): 65.

cultural identity or can be posed, in the case of personal identity, in terms of interpersonal relationships. Such concerns are unavoidable in this era of pluralistic, classless, multicultural open societies. People have always discerned their identities in company with others, but the shared worldview of close neighbors is a thing of the past. Diversity apparently favors dispersion more than integration. Yet diversity also promotes an opening to others, and wider horizons. Pedagogical thought from the time of the Greeks has regarded travel as beneficial because exposure to other peoples and cultures leads to an expansion of spirit, while forming the mind and the affections.

Family life is an introduction to diversity in an environment of coexistence where people tend to agree on large goals while disagreeing on daily issues. Diversity of sex and age also is a given in the family. Contact with parents, brothers and sisters, and other relatives leads to a continuous opening to diversity, even more intense than in society because it occurs in intimate relationships. Family coexistence protects and promotes the discovery of one's own identity within the framework of the relationships with others. Development proceeds naturally, not artificially. In this way, sociability is expanded and consolidated through coexistence as a way of life.

5.3 Educational framework of personal relationships

In light of what has been said, family education can be seen as a form of influence that relies on proposing rather than formal teaching. This, however, is a "strong" influence that operates continually, not just now and then, and impacts on the formation of human personality. It is an important element in practical coexistence, since within the family the individual members are treated as persons. This popularly is called *love*. For parents there is nobody like their children, and for children, there is nobody like their parents; and this too is what we call love.

Love and the personal approach are simply different expressions of recognition of the dignity of the human being, esteemed for himself. This happens naturally in the family, and it is natural for two simple reasons: because it takes place not in words but in actions, and because it is not a fruit of reflection but of elemental love, of a radical donation and acceptance. Family coexistence is a web of individual relationships or, from an anthropological view, an educational framework of interpersonal relationships. This is the natural character of the family.

Here then is the necessary perspective for understanding in all its depth the feature of the family that is often said to define it in relation to other institutions: kinship bonds. Kinship is established by consanguinity and is based on biological generation. This does not rule out the possibility that in some instances, families with adopted members also may be settings for authentic family relations—though in these cases interpersonal relationships are analogously modeled on those of other families. There also are organizations in which people treat each other as family, and these can be called "families" too. This is particularly true where the "children" of such a family have a kind of spiritual, rather than biological, begetting. Despite their differences, the variety of family forms found through the ages all support deep personal relationships. This is why the family is debased and destroyed when interpersonal relationships are abandoned. Indeed, if these are merely neglected, a slow and silent deterioration takes place over time.

The interpersonal relationships that constitute the family reveal the dialogical nature of the human being. The truism that love requires deeds and not just words is fully confirmed in the family. From the love of his parents the child perceives who he is, discovers his roots, and discerns his identity. Recognizing oneself as son or daughter opens the way to sociability in relationships of giving and receiving with brothers and sisters, grandparents and other relatives within an environment of friendship. This is a fertile source of socialization for the individual.

Here then is the essence of family education: a function, yes, the practice of daily living together as a family. From this totally free, interpersonal network of relationships arise individual and social responsibility. The family is a vehicle for the lifelong humanizing process that every person must experience. It has much to do with civilization. A lot has been written about the "noble savage," but although he may exhibit great nobility, nevertheless he remains a savage. Civilization's faults do not obscure its marvelous achievements; and along with some really inhuman actions one finds noble and superior deeds that might not have been found a few centuries, or even a few decades ago. These are fruits of civilization. For example, the Universal Declaration of Human Rights, though ignored in many places, unquestionably provides a point of reference for relationships between societies.

The family is the beginning of civilization, in each person and in humankind in general. And it is not only the beginning but a permanent principle.

5.4. Confidence, sociability, and solidarity

Interpersonal relationships are grounded in a profoundly human attitude that is frequently forgotten: *confidence.* Yet social dealings seem to be infused with lack of trust and to illustrate the truth of the pessimistic saying "*Think the worst and you will be right.*"

The crass individualism of modern liberal thinking directs this suspicion against other individuals seen as potential threats to our personal projects. There is in fact no room for confidence in liberal individualism, since it regards others only as *others*—that is, different and opposed. The possibility of acts of giving and receiving does not exist. Yet the summit of all human relationships, as we have seen, is interpersonal relationship, in which individuals are recognized as persons, and community is forged. Giving and receiving things is not enough for this to happen; it is necessary to give oneself and accept the other. Liberal individualism makes this impossible, inasmuch as others are strangers and possible friends are traveling companions at best.

This is why the recent criticism of liberal individualism turns to the family as an intermediate community. The aim is to recover the human sense of social relationships manifested in the mutual attention and care of family members. Psychological and educational research indicates that direct participation by parents in the education of their children is an essential component of fruitful education, so much so that other elements lose their effectiveness without it. There is a near-unanimous consensus that the kind of relationships found in a family have a positive effect on the child's self-perception and feelings of security; if these relationships are absent, affective instability results. There is also agreement that confidence nurtured in the family does more to promote personal security in the ethical and psychological spheres than any other motivating factor, whether intrinsic or extrinsic.

Confidence or trust is a fundamental element in human interaction, with a rich variety of significant, and sometimes slightly confusing, features. It is first of all a part of that personal giving and receiving that involves a certain equity but no repayment and is never demanded but always acknowledged with thanks. It is the relational aspect of human love, the source of the security that people, especially children, need and that serves as a buffer against the sharp edges of social relationships. Confidence is also one of the most difficult attitudes to generate and maintain, especially in formation efforts.

It is understandable that people seek a certain uniformity in educational outcomes and their correspondence to an ideal of education. Yet attempts to mold individuals in specific ways may not suit the personalities of the learners. When that is so, disappointing results may give rise to discouragement, with a resulting loss of confidence by the educator that undermines the confidence of the child. Suspicion and shyness then are likely to smother the natural tendency to sociability.

The perception of their children as unique and irreplaceable gives parents the moral and psychic energy to persevere confidently. Tendencies more noble than sociability, like generosity and altruism, emerge and become positive habits. This is the origin of social or "public" virtues, such as affability and veracity, often lacking today. Sharp edges and guile in social contacts block the growth of community and the practice of giving and receiving in interpersonal relationships; but the experience of mutual trust offers a key for the development of sociability. It is beyond the reach of even the best school to teach it if it has not first put down roots in the family.

5.5. *Freedom and affectivity*

Freedom is an essential part of education. It is a source of interior energy that orients one to the surrounding world and to life with others. More than just removing external obstacles, freedom supports the intimate aspirations that lead to fulfillment. Genuine freedom, then, is not "freedom from . . . " but "freedom for . . . " The project for doing what is good and avoiding what is evil, never finally realized but always open, requires an informed evaluation of capacities and goals. Choosing will be powerfully hampered without a suitable emotional life allowing one to assess one's possibilities and avoid the lure of immediate gratification. The proper exercise of freedom lies in regulating one's behavior so that one can say, "I do what I want"—really want, that is.

Attaining this fulfillment of human dignity is hard, indeed materially impossible for many, due to a lack of minimal resources and means. Others will experience frustration, arising from the renunciations demanded by authentic freedom. Yet failure has particularly painful consequences in the area of social relationships—a lack of responsibility leads to an increased individualism and decreased sociability.

Freedom, then, is not a quality to be expanded, but a task to be performed. The family is the original environment for its strengthening and growth, with maturation in the future in other fields—professional work, social relationships, even free time (time for doing what I really want to do).

To realize the task of freedom it is necessary to develop control over emotions that may distract us from our deepest motives. Preparation for the mature exercise of control begins in early infancy, mainly through the development of habits of moderation followed by the formation of fortitude. The tendency to unfocused activity is first overcome, followed by the fear in the face of obstacles and difficulties opposed to our existential projects.

The role of the family is essential in the education of affectivity. The choice of a child about candy must be moderated as much as an adolescent's choice about the use of free time. In both cases, the goal is to remedy undesirable tendencies: from gluttony in infancy, to sloth in adolescence. But education must employ different tactics depending on age or, better, individual development. The pedagogical aim should not be some notion of "good behavior" as determined by what is politically correct but should suit the intimate demands of each developing personality. If carried out in this way, education of affectivity in infancy and adolescence will bear its fullest fruit in maturity and will be a decisive factor in the opening to superior values like commitment, tolerance, and solidarity.

This educational mission belongs in the family due to its superior resources and more suitable goals. As a framework of interpersonal relationships, the family allows more freedom for emotions than the school can offer. The school can reinforce the education of affectivity as it is lived naturally in the family, but it cannot replace it.

6. THE BASIC PRIORITY OF EDUCATION IN THE FAMILY

The distinction between formal, nonformal, and informal education has been familiar in pedagogical literature since the conclusions of the International Conference on the Crisis in Education held in Williamsburg, Virginia in 1967. These conclusions, published one year later, are still used in pedagogical discourse.[22] The distinction involves a positive valuation of institutional education—so-called formal education from school to university—in relation to informal education, including family education. The success of this distinction, which favors formal education, has paradoxically caused the criticisms that prompted it to be forgotten. These criticisms can be summed up as two abuses and one insufficiency.

a) The school (formal education) is assigned an unjustified central role the education of the person, as if it were the principal and nearly unique educational agent.

b) Due to this false emphasis, the real significance of other agents in human formation is obscured.

c) In fact, the methods and procedures of formal education cannot keep up with the needs of a culture in continuous transformation.

Although these points were made forty years ago, the errors they capsulize have increased. "Educational system" is used to designate formal and even nonformal education (educational activities organized outside the official academic system), while family education is ignored or discounted.

---

22. P. H. Coombs, *La crisis mundial de la educación* (New York: Oxford University Press, 1968).

Common experience nevertheless testifies that the learning decisive for the formation of the human personality is that which takes place within the family. It can be the source of some psychological pathologies, as Freud maintained, but it is also responsible for the fundamental orientations that shape basic attitudes in the opening to reality. D. Goleman says "No matter how much we try to convince ourselves of the contrary, we all carry the stamp of the emotional habits learned in our relationship with our parents."[23] It is hardly a surprise that growing interest in the education of affectivity has fostered a rediscovery of the value of family education—informal but hardly inconsequential—as the place where affectivity begins.

It could not be otherwise. The family is the natural setting for education and the original framework of interpersonal relationships. Within the family an individual is truly a person because he is considered, treated, and appreciated as such—valued and affirmed for being as he is, not on intellectual grounds but because of the acceptance that comes with being loved. As Joseph Pieper points out, to love somebody means approving him: "to turn one's face to him and say: it is good that you exist, it is good that you be in the world."[24] This approval, says Pieper, is not intellectual assent or an effusion of emotional sympathy, but an act of the will. It is important to avoid the intellectualism that can lead one to imagine that reasoned reflection by itself will move one to treat others as persons.

Historian Paul Johnson points out that modern tyrants, especially those of the twentieth century, while basing their power on the expectation of an imminent utopia, nevertheless did not hesitate to destroy individuals and even whole populations.[25] They justified this by appealing to the salvation of

23. D. Goleman, *Inteligencia emocional* (Barcelona: Kairós, 1995): 232.

24. J. Pieper, *Amor*, in *Las virtudes fundamentales* (Madrid: Rialp, 1997): 436.

25. Cf. P. Johnson, *Tiempos modernos* (Buenos Aires: Javier Vergara, ed., 1988).

humanity or a significant part of it—nation, social class, race. Evidently one can "love" humanity in general terms, while at the same time, hating particular humans. Rational recognition of the supreme value of the person can coexist with arbitrarily declaring some to be *non-persons*, as often happens these days. For example: the defense of human life, carried on with unparalleled vigor, except when it is a question of unborn life.

These are dark days, but there is no knowing whether the changes now being experienced by the family will bring any improvement. It depends on human actions of a political, cultural, and juridical nature. Above everything else, however, the family can be, as it has been originally and always, a genuine source of education. Family policies truly beneficial to the family must begin from this insight: the need that the family be faithful to itself and recover its original form so as simply to be what it is.

CHAPTER 2

COEXISTENCE IN THE FAMILY:
*Developing Personal Identity**

(Francisco Altarejos, Alfredo Rodríguez, Aurora Bernal)

The need to celebrate anniversaries sheds light on essential human dimensions of sociability and culture. A celebration is a *commemoration*, that is, the joyful sharing of a memory by a group. There is no celebrating or commemorating alone. These festivities are reminders that several people have something in common: certain values, an important past event, something whose recalling causes joy. (The memory of sorrows evokes mourning.) The celebration of the tenth anniversary of the United Nations' 1994 International Year of the Family[1] is an appropriate occasion for again reflecting on the reality of the family. As is generally recognized, too, the proclamation by the UN of an International Year on this or that is a way of sensitizing and mobilizing international political organs and all organs

---

* This chapter is based on two papers: Altarejos, F. and Rodríguez, A. (2004), "Identidad, coexistencia y familia," *Estudios sobre educación*, 6, 105–118; Altarejos, F., Rodríguez, A, Bernal, A. (2004). "La familia, forja de la sociabilidad: aceptación y donación" (Comunicación), II Congreso Internacional de la Familia, *La familia, el futuro de la sociedad*, Palma de Mallorca, 22, 23, 24 de noviembre.

1. The UN organ responsible for following up on the program elaborated in connection with this commemoration is the División for Social Policy and Development in the Department of Economic and Social Affairs.

of society. In the present instance, a re-evaluation of the social function of the family is taking place which takes note of new problems of the last ten years.

1. SOCIABILITY AND SOCIALIZATION

Relationships between family and society are difficult to analyze with any degree of precision. We can start with the bonds that lead to *sociability* and *socialization*. Sociability refers directly to the social education of the human being, socialization to the influence of the environment upon the individual. Neither concept can be separated from the unity of the person.

First of all, one should notice that "we are all born sociable, but not social, in a strict sense. . . . We are born sociable, but not social, in the same way that we are born educable but not educated."[2] Education is needed to acquire personal maturity (sociability) as a foundation for living—with, that is, the capacity to perform positive social acts.

Durkheim is a good source for understanding socialization. For him, "education is the action exercised by adult generations over those who have not yet attained the degree of maturity necessary for social life. It attempts to develop in the child a certain number of physical, intellectual, and moral traits demanded by political society and the specific environment to which he is destined."[3] It is not the same as sociability (a quality of the human being empowering him to express himself in society) and socialization (an external consequence of education).

Two aspects of each person's education deserve notice here. We must know the human condition and cultivate social virtues (sociability), while at the same time acquiring familiarity with the social environment (socialization). Attention to

2. J. L. García Garrido, *Los fundamentos de la educación social* (Madrid: EMESA, 1971): 106.

3. E. Durkheim, *Educación y sociología* (Barcelona: Península, 1996): 50.

both is required for authentic education and social improvement. If social education is considered simply in relation to adaptation to the environment, we are obliged to conclude that it diminishes the person, whether by over-abstractness or excessive concreteness.

On the other hand, if attention is directed only to the natural social tendency of the individual, integration into an environment is likely to be unstable and weak. Personal development and social maturity are not possible without attending to one's surroundings. Social education cannot be undifferentiated and uniform; it is essential to take into consideration the unique differences among individuals. Inequality must be taken into account as an element of socialization, not to do away with it but in order to acknowledge the individuality of individuals and address the different needs of different environments. Social virtues must be acquired for the sake of true living together. Equity in education does not mean leveling all differences, but enabling each one to achieve the best of which he is capable in his particular environment. This is the rich meaning of what can be called "learning to be."[4]

2. SOCIAL DIMENSION OF FAMILY EDUCATION

People are social by nature. They cannot live comfortably in solitude but must develop their capacity for social interaction with others. A man therefore truly finds himself only in giving in self-donation. At the same time, man is a seeker who searches for personal identity. Other identities—social, professional, familial, sexual—end in emptiness. But this emptiness, which is the emptiness of deconstructionism, is necessary to

---

4. Cf. J. Delhors, eds, *La educación encierra un tesoro* (Madrid: Santillana-Ediciones, UNESCO, 1996).

the extent that it stimulates a constructive process of examining the diverse identities so as to find the answer to the question: who am I? Deconstruction construction is the social process in which people for the last several decades have found themselves engaged.

The tendency to social interaction in the family is not selective but is open without discriminatory diversity. In fact, this is a kind of referential openness. Acceptance of others—parents, brothers and sisters, grandparents, uncles, cousins, etc.—is the starting point of natural human sociability and individual socialization. Ought not the strengthening of socialization in the family or, more directly, strengthening the family itself to be promoted as the sure way of socializing society? Yet as matters stand, the family is commonly thought to be a community dependent on and subservient to society. The problem is not so much that this idea is mistaken as that it ignores a crucial element—sociability, the tendency to interact socially.

Among the issues investigated at the United Nations, presented as hints to governments and other bodies concerned with family life, family functions are cited under the heading of socialization and social welfare.[5] Studies increasingly confirm a weakening in these matters. Other problems are considered side by side with this one, although no causal relationship is established nor is any effort made to probe more deeply—desirable though this would be—in order to discover possible relationships among the symptoms of family pathology. There is a mere anxious citing of things like declining birth rates, population aging, the spread of AIDS, and changes in family structure, as elements in the current perplexity about what a family is.[6]

---

5. UN General Assembly, *Preparation for the Tenth Anniversary of the International Year of the Family in 2004*, No. 57/139, 17 July 2002 (A/57/139): no. 9–12.

6. H. Bradon, *Major Trends Affecting Families Worldwide*, in *Family Matters*, 45, (August, 2003) Bulletin of the International Year of the Family. It can be found in *http://www.un.org/esa/socdev/family/Publications/FamilyMatters/(2004 March)*.

Analyses are based on empirical studies. Indicators that help the evaluation are concerned with material and emotional well-being. There are no moral judgments, since the methodology does not allow for them. The emphasis is on establishing facts and encouraging a search for solutions, generously assumed to reside in the allocation of more material resources.

The urgent need to strengthen solidarity between the generations is emphasized, with the stress on care of children and seniors. Two concepts, socialization and education, figure in this analysis, with the first taken as primary.[7] Socialization is understood as adaptation to society, learned originally in the family; it needs reinforcing inasmuch as contemporary society is in constant flux, due either to harmful factors or to positive progress. Change may lead to a more complex society with improved living conditions and a better future for all. Education is understood as schooling by which people acquire basic competence for life.[8] Other suggestions in recent UN declarations deal with the relationship between the strengthening of family values and social cohesion.[9]

Among the Non-Governmental Organizations that support the UN, the work of the National Council of Family Relations—NCFR—should be noted for its research.[10]

This body has promoted knowledge about the family for almost seventy years and thereby contributed to family well-being.[11] Reviewing the working of this organization suggest how the issue of sociability in the family is seen by the international community.

---

7. UN General Assembly, *Preparation for the Tenth Anniversary*, no. 5–6.

8. UN Department of Economic and Social Affairs, *Preparation for the Tenth Anniversary of the International Year of the Family in 2004*. Report of the Secretary General, 41st session, 10–21. February, 2003 (E/CN.5/2003/6): no. 5.

9. UN General Assembly, *Preparation for the Tenth Anniversary*, no. 7.

10. Ibid., no. 51.

11. A. Bernal, *"Hace diez años,"* 83–85.

3. THE STUDY OF SOCIABILITY WITHIN THE FAMILY

Sociological and psychological research by NCFR focuses on the individual and his material and emotional welfare. There is a corresponding emphasis on educational and labor opportunities. But some family issues have been set aside, including choice of mate, religion, the power and enrichment of the family and the extended family. Research is ongoing on the quality of marriages, the relationship of work and family, and divorce and its consequences. What is new is the attention devoted to issues such as paternity, family structure, violence, the development of persons at different ages, and increasingly, studies dealing with adolescents and seniors.[12] The studies embrace a broad sample of persons of different races, socio-economic status, and sexual orientation. Generalizations about the family based on limited samples are deplored.[13]

Sociability, the tendency to social interaction, comes up peripherally in the consideration of other issues that have some relationship with it. It is not given specific consideration, however, in reference to intra-family processes like marital interaction, domestic violence, relationships between fathers, mothers, sons and daughters, brothers and sisters, grandparents, etc. Although the point of view appears to be holistic, the deep significance of sociability goes unrecognized due to the emphasis on individual fulfillment in preference to interpersonal relations (critical to understanding the family, as we shall see in Chapter 4). There is repeated attention to the question of how individuals work out their identities. Family relationships are studied exclusively from the individual perspective; interaction

---

12. R. M. Milardo, "Preface. The Decade in Review," in *Understanding Families. Into the New Millennium: A Decade in Review* (Lawrence: NCFR, 2001): vii–ix.

13. S. Coontz, "Historical Perspectives on Family Studies," in Milardo, R. M., ed., *Understanding Families. Into the New Millennium: A Decade in Review* (Lawrence: NCFR, 2001): 80–94.

is overlooked. Family structure is deemed important, but the focus is always on its external, measurable aspects. And even here an attempt is made to determine the quality of family relationships by material criteria that include, among others, purchasing power.

The sort of a study that devotes closest attention to the sociability fostered in a family may be that which examines affectivity and emotional states, especially when sociability is taken as signifying acceptance of the others and adaptation to membership in a group. There is research that shows that stable, long-lasting love for their children makes people better adapted to society. Children's emotional welfare depends on a positive relationship between their parents, which in turn nurture support and fair discipline. Once this is settled, other problems, like the economic ones, can be resolved.[14]

The subject of sociability also emerges in the analysis of various educational styles and notice is frequently given to the solidarity seen in families from cultures different from the Anglo-American such as those of Asian and Hispanic origin. Thus, as the promotion of individual autonomy is seen as the key to the development of individuals in the United States, in these other types of families values are promoted which are more suitable to socialization, the authors say, such as cooperation, reciprocity, and interdependence.[15]

In studies of families with limited economic resources (often, immigrant families), the contribution of the family as community is noted. This involves goals that go beyond the satisfaction of the individual, although relevant to it. At the same time, the influence of the community on family dynamics has been studied. A growing number of studies show the relationship

---

14. D. H. Demo, M. J. Cox, "Families in the Middle and Later Years: A Review and Critique of Research in the 1990s," in Milardo, ed., *Understanding Families. Into the New Millennium: A Decade in Review* (Lawrence: NCFR, 2001): 98.

15. Ibid., 103.

between family types and success in the schooling of children who must adapt, as must their parents, to a different culture, language, and mores. Experience of and reinforcement from the community are quite positive.[16] And it has been shown that family openness to other social groups or associations favors the socialization of individuals, when this process is understood as integration and adaptation.[17]

Another way of illustrating the treatment of sociability in current family studies is by examining social policies concerning the family as community. Political theory is critical of the damage to public life brought about by an exaggerated individualism. This criticism began in the 1980s but increased in the 1990s. The idea is that the family is best understood as a community, not just as the individuals that form it, by taking note of its place in the wider society.[18]

The crisis of individual identity coincides with the crisis of social participation, since in both perspectives a deficiency in the area of interpersonal relations is at the heart of the problem. The debate between neoliberals and communitarians raised the issue of family involvement and social participation. The relationship between identity and sociability, often equated with socialization, continues to be debated in political theory, especially in its anthropological and ethical dimensions.

Sociology looks at this issue under the banner of *social capital*. From a sociology at the service of the economy, but transcending it and considering far larger issues than mere productivity, Coleman studies the family from the point of view

16. S. Walker, D. Riley, "Involvement of the Personal Social Network as a Factor in Parent Education Effectiveness," in *Family Relations*, 50, (2), (2001): 186–193.

17. C. Delgado-Gaitán, "School Matters in the Mexican-American Home: Socializing Children to Education," in *American Educational Research Journal*, 29 (3), (1992): 504.

18. K. Bogenschneider, "Has Family Policy Come of Age? A Decade Review of the State of U.S. Family Policy in the 1990s," in Milardo, ed., *Understanding Families. Into the New Millennium*, 358.

of education. The thesis is simple: People find resources to help them in their work and living in their relations with others. Expectation, confidence, the acceptance of norms and obligations—fundamental elements in interpersonal relationships—help to improve functioning.

In this perspective dating to the end of the 1980s one finds an interesting approach to the study of sociability that reflects the whole of human reality: what is individual cannot be understood without reference to social life and vice-versa. The family is an environment where this relationship can be observed. And in doing so it becomes clear that parental financial resources and educational level do not have a positive influence on children if the children do not interact with their parents. The physical presence of parents is necessary.[19] Intra-family relationships can be supported in the schools and by the community. Research into these realities is increasing.[20]

Coleman's suggestions have influenced empirical research on family issues that differs from most studies and points to a deeper meaning of sociability. One may suppose this author and his followers to recognize that growing up in a family enriches personality, through the opening up to others that results. This insight into the close bond between personal and social development can be glimpsed in the penultimate statement of the United Nations, which stresses the family as a community and learning environment where the social responsibility of its members takes root and grows. The implication is

19. J. S. Coleman, "Social Capital in the Creation of Human Capital," in *American Journal of Sociology* 94, (1988): Supplement, 111.

20. R. Crosnoe, "Social Capital and the Interplay of Families and Schools," in *Journal of Marriage and Family* 66 (5), (2004): 267–280. A. Farrell, C. Tayler, L. Tennent, "Building Social Capital in Early Childhood Education and Care: An Australian Study," in *British Educational Research Journal* 30 (5), (2004): 623–633.

that the family perspective must be taken into consideration in relation to all social problems.[21]

4. THE CONCEPT OF IDENTITY

Ever present and never resolved among social problems is the problem of identity. Life goes faster and faster. People frequently are called to act at once, with insufficient information. Haste gives rise to error—as one sees in the widespread terminological confusion and simplified arguments employed in discussions of identity. Globalization, considered by the United Nations one of the main trends transforming families in our times, supplies the background of this confusion.[22]

From one point of view, globalization can be seen as an efficient way of developing the human aspiration to universality. The discovery of this opening to universality began centuries ago around the Mediterranean. But its elaboration has required hard work and, after more than twenty centuries, still does. Ethnocentrism, the tendency to make one's own culture the exclusive norm for evaluating the behavior of other groups, races, or societies, is a socio-cultural way of affirming personal identity that blocks the opening to universality and, from the sociological perspective, does harm to the family. Even now, it is the temptation to view others as "barbarians" that constitutes the greatest obstacle to the universality of human sympathy. It is necessary to start with a clear understanding of what is meant by identity. Leaving aside the dictionary meaning, two other basic senses are pertinent to this discussion.[23]

---

21. UN Department of Economic and Social Affairs. Session Dec. 10–12, 2003, in *http://www.un.org/esa/socdev/family* [Disponible, IX, 2004], 1–4.

22. Cf. F. Altarejos, A. Rodríguez, J. Fontrodona, *Retos educativos de la globalización. Hacia una sociedad solidaria* (Pamplona: Astrolabio, EUNSA, 2003), especially cf. cap. VI.

23. Cf. H. Esquer, *El límite del pensamiento. La propuesta metodológica de Leonardo Polo* (Pamplona: EUNSA, 2000): 167–168.

a) Identity as a general value. This is the modern concept of identity, originating with Hegel. It is realized as identification, subjective submission to objective values that characterize one. These begin as mere description, but, following affiliation with a group that they define, one becomes linked to that group and alienated from those not part of it. The person dissolves in abstractions considered to be supreme values for humanity as a whole, not just for the group. ("If they were like us, there would be no problems.")

b) Identity as reference to origin. Identity is understood as an actualization of one's point of origin. I do not define myself by affiliation with a group but by filiation, the original belonging, partially expressed in a tradition summing up the sources of my existence— family, mother country, language, culture, religion. Perfecting myself does not lie in self-affirmation or a narrow-minded apologia for my group, but in the intense and daily experience of living with others.

Which is the predominant sense of identity now? Without doubt, the first: identity understood as a general value, which in addition is posited as the foundation of my being. In the classic way of thinking, the role of principle or foundation was assigned to nature. The increased prominence of autonomy and subjectivity in modern thought makes the human spirit the protagonist. Man himself determines and explains everything, controls everything, can do as he wants in relation to everything.

As we have pointed out on another occasion, "Here is the problematic kernel of the notion of identity: a willingness to accept the fact that people do not create themselves, so that freedom is not the ultimate starting point of their existence and their personal identity is not a product of a rationally thought-out process that begins in abstract values . . . . Identity is . . . fundamentally something one receives and . . .

develops in communicating and living with others. Thus freedom . . . opens one to others and supplies rational justification for such opening."[24]

Identity is realized in persons living in an environment: society. This does not happen by a process of reasoning or willing, but through an unfolding of the self in a variety of experiences of existing with others and becoming open to them. It leads to an opening up to the *universal*, not the *general*. The difference is essential. The "general" is that which is common to a genus; whereas "universal" signifies a unity within the diversity of reality.

Often diversity is judged a nuisance, inasmuch as it highlights unique features that impede generalization. But universality is an empty concept if it treats diversity as something abstract, to be absorbed in the quest for unity. The authentic aspiration to universality affirms what is singular and particular, since diversity offers valuable clues to something which is shared in common at the deepest human level, namely, the radical humanity of the human person. In this way, identity and universality are established as complementary poles of human relationships.

5. AFFIRMATION OF IDENTITY

The modern sense of identity is totally opposed to the radical giving and receiving of which human beings are capable. If "identity" derives from one's identifying with a group and its specific values and individuality, then others can only be perceived as potential threats, inasmuch as the resulting dependence seems to be in conflict with the autonomy one desires. Identity and universality are then opposed. But if we understand identity in reference to the origin of one's being, then the affirmation of identity

---

24. F. Altarejos, A. Rodríguez, J. Fontrodona, *Retos educativos de la globalización*, 166.

is certainly opposed to the aspiration of universality. Each, however, needs the other. The relationship is complementary. Identity, then, is not seen as deriving from self-awareness and involvement with a group, but as something that is discovered in the encounter with other identities—in mutual acceptance and dependence—brought about by a desire for universality.

From the consideration of original identity, we draw several conclusions.

- If identity refers to origin, then it is a received identity, one that is largely a given. Identity, then, is not only or mainly a derivative of individual autonomy.

- Received identity must not be understood as a static fact, an unchangeable destiny, but as a starting point. Beginning there, one shapes one's life in openness to the future.

- If identity is a matter of origin, a personal identity comes with having been born a unique being. Part of it are the familial, cultural, and national identities that take shape from being born and growing up among particular people and interacting with them. At the same time, one also identifies with all human beings, free persons like ourselves. Here is the basic opening to others.

Original identity thus contains the seed of universality. Common origin implies an opening up that overcomes the individualism of an identity closed on itself: identity is not a limitation but an opening to the whole of humanity. Identity and universality are not seen as opposed, but as complementary poles of a relationship. This is a rich source of meaning for education—and for considering the family as an educational agent.

Ultimately, education is directed to the affirmation and realization of general values by the student, whose formation and learning constitutes a process of adaptation to those objective elements. In this analysis, educator and pupil are merely "individuals" in reference to a value system and a group—source of authentic identity—which includes all the general values.

6. PERSONAL BEING AND COEXISTENCE

Openness to the other, self-giving, being-with—these are fundamental characteristics of the human person that he is incapable of giving up. Being-with is not just a juxtaposition of existences that establishes peace between alien existences often perceived as opposed. In this limited sense of "coexistence" differences are tolerated provided they do not challenge the generic values that define one's identity. Tolerance can indeed be one of the values of an identity system that implies coexistence; but the latter is understood as a mere juxtaposition of existences that does not finally require accepting others. Where tolerance is a supreme value, intolerance is unacceptable; but accepting another as part of a group is not the same as welcoming him, and tolerating his existence is not the same as regarding it, precisely because it is diverse; as complementary to my own. From this point of view, diversity is far more than an "enriching" factor; it is a dynamic factor in the development and shaping of one's own identity.

Being in relationship with other persons, then, is not a mere supplement to one's personhood, but the essence of personal existence, which needs other people to fully realize itself. To live with others is not thereby reduced to the satisfaction of needs nor to the fostering of dialogue as a way to mutual understanding. The perfecting of one's existence instead requires the existence of another person, just as the other's perfecting requires one's own. This is the fundamental goal of being-with: mutual perfecting and acceptance. It takes place most fully in the family. One may not be accepted in a professional or social setting, but that cannot happen in a family, for then it would cease being such and become a sort of mutual benefit association. Filiation is precisely what constitutes me as a person. I cannot renounce it, because it does not depend on me. Depersonalization is not just emptiness or the absence of fulfilling social relationships. A depersonalized existence is the product of renunciation of self-improvement or a radical separation of self-improvement from the improvement of others. Every form of segregation is directly opposed to the person and the experience of living with others, which is fundamental to personhood. Family breakdown is thus a grave attack on personal identity and the tendency to be in social relationships, with inevitable consequences for general social health. The radical acceptance of living with others involves self-giving, similarly radical.

We are not dealing here only with giving but with giving oneself. Giving must involve giving oneself and accepting the other. Father and mother give themselves and accept the child. Giving by itself is not enough: those who only give things to their children may fulfill the social function of the family but do not realize its essential mission of fostering the mutual happiness of its members. This requires accepting, without which the giving makes no sense. Spaemann has stated correctly that "acceptance is the key to making someone's identity a reality for others: to accept the other, we must experience his identity in loving and being loved."[25] This is how self-giving works hand in hand with the intimate and inseparable acceptance of the other. Here is the essence of human social interaction.

This is often forgotten in charitable campaigns of various sorts. The effort is made to evoke compassionate feelings, but that limits the scope of the response. The immediate reaction may be a financial contribution, but the response remains on the level of superficial and ephemeral feelings.

---

25. R. Spaemann, *Personas. Acerca de la distinción entre algo y alguien* (Pamplona: EUNSA, 2000): 89.

Authentic giving must involve the whole person, acting through the will, and giving not merely things but himself, through the things he gives. The natural environment where such social interaction is forged and self-giving is fostered is the family, within which giving and accepting take place naturally.

7. THE FAMILY AS CRADLE OF PERSONAL COEXISTENCE

Possibly the greatest obstacle to a proper understanding and appreciation of the family is the limited frame of reference employed by today's sociological and psychological analysis. As we have seen, the limitations are epistemological in origin—they concern knowledge. The family is a highly complex reality that resists the division and separation of analysis. Some aspects may be adequately treated by an analytical method, but there can be no complete, holistic explanation apart from recognition of the family's complexity. Its starting point is what is naturally experienced, viewed prior to rational formalization.

Common experience testifies with certainty that living with others, which defines the person, is realized in family life in a natural way, without the need to give a self-conscious account of the actions of family members. A child does not need to reflect on who his father and mother are. He recognizes them as such, accepts them, and lives with them. All the positive characteristics of identity and living with others, subject as they are to anthropological reflection, can be seen to be ordinary aspects of living.

To begin with, the identity of each member of a family is established from the first moment, as something he is born with. In addition, human generation does not end with birth; it is followed by the sustenance and education that parents provide for their children. St. Thomas Aquinas states: "Children love their parents as a highest good, because they are their main benefactors, insofar as they are the source of their existence, of their food, and of their education."[26] In this continuity of diverse acts we find an anthropological subtext, which has to be coexistence, understood as radical or transcendental of the person. Only the idea of living with another or others can serve as a principle to bring together procreation, the need for food, and the convenience of education. The profound unity here can be understood only in light of the giving and receiving required by living-with. Here is what makes the family, understood from a social perspective, the basic cell of society, which other institutions cannot replace but can only complement inasmuch as it is the point of origin of the person. When there is no family, the point of origin is lost. This is how children end up in the hands of welfare agencies or adoption agencies, which then attempt to supply them with an environment that will resemble a family as much as possible, without being one.

Naturally, then, there is an intimate bond between identity and living with others. Identity is not some kind of universal value, and the newborn child and infant cannot "identify" himself with anything: totally dependent on his parents, he is unable to constitute or construct his identity for himself. Thus, living with others is an existential act or radical structural component of the person who, from his intimate self, opens up to the closest co-existential bonding between parents and children.

The unquestionable mutual need—nutritional in children, affective in parents—is not exhausted, as would be the case if freedom were taken to be unbounded independence and maximum autonomy in individual decision-making. The levels of adult existence are prefigured in those of infancy; growth does not reject but develops and perfects these latter. The living-with of infancy is a clue to the insight that autonomy is a relative

---

26. Thomas Aquinas, *In VIII Ethicorum*, 1. 12, n. 1715. Cf. A. Millán-Puelles, *La formación de la personalidad humana* (Madrid: Rialp, 1963): 18ff.

value, and not one of preeminent importance, as often supposed. More than being autonomous, it is important to be with others; more than living independently, it is necessary to receive and give. This does not exclude autonomy, since each person is his own developing project, with a real autonomy springing from the original dependence of filiation in the family, which lasts throughout the person's life.

This phenomenon of living with others points directly to another aspect of human relationships, clearly visible in the family: openness to diversity, that is, to the life project of each arising from his self-acceptance and shaped by his uniqueness and inimitability. Openness to intimacy is also openness to intimacy with diverse persons, enriching by reason of each one's novelty. Within the common framework of human nature one finds fundamental differences resting upon diversity in the context of living together.

Beginning with the difference of age between parent and child, the development of persons expands in relationships with other family members, brothers and sisters first of all and then other relatives. Each different person within a family is a concrete incarnation of diversity, linked to others by origin. Here is the first opening to universality experienced by the person; occurring just after the end of lactation, it is an experiential knowledge needing no abstract formulae or citing of intangible general values. From that experience one moves on to abstract knowledge and to other types of communities, more or less distant from the experience of common origin. Thus one passes from the family to the clan and, later, to the tribe.

In this process one counters the experience of alienation from others who are generally qualitatively different from oneself. It can be dangerous in groups larger than clan or tribe—for instance, the nation or the state. When one returns to life in the environment that lies close at hand, one is likely to find it no longer open but a space closed to strangers. A nation, as repository of a culture and concrete social tendencies, tends to close in on itself and to view transcultural relations with mistrust: the state, in the end, is only the receptacle for appropriate kinds of individuals formed for citizenship within families. The state ought to serve both families and individuals, and to do so for their benefit, of course, but also and above all for its own benefit as repository of values. In contrast, in the family the opening to diversity is realized naturally through receiving and giving in relations with other people, each one unique but all with the same origin. Without need of formal teaching, the family as educator communicates that unity and diversity are not only possible but necessary. Children learn that complementarity, not mere tolerance, is the preferred route to a satisfactory experience of living with others. It is much more, a coexistence in which the ethical glue comes from receiving and giving. The experience originates in the radical difference between the sexes, so that the family is grounded in the union of two people who complement each other: this man and this woman are open to the arrival of others who replicate and expand the difference between them—their children.

Today, however, one finds people speaking of "family models," admitting without a second thought that there are families in which sexual difference is irrelevant, and basing the family simply upon a decision to enter into a contract. This is the position of some sociologists and psychologists. It is easy to see why those who think like this oppose placing obstacles in the way of any sort of life in common that involves a sharing of bed and board and bears some resemblance to a family.

From this perspective, too, it follows logically that "sexual orientation" cannot constitute an impediment, since otherwise the right to individual freedom and identity is violated. Identity is thought to be an individual or social construct, not something related to origin. In the end, it makes no difference whether identity is assembled by individuals, society, or both.

Identity is a product of ideas and general values, and choices among them. Relativism springs from these ideas. And not just ethical relativism, which in the end retains some norms of behavior, reflecting real-world experience. Here, rather, we confront cultural relativism, which looks for its confirmation to a future in which some ideas will persist and others will grow weak and disappear. So, for instance, the idea of "family models" is associated with the idea of "gender" viewed by some as altogether different from biological sex that imposes limits on the supreme good of individual freedom. Sex, an original element of personal identity, must be overcome through the "construction" of gender as the main element of identity, and one constructed on the basis of freedom of choice.

And so the gap is closed between what we will and what we can do. Being a man or a woman used to be an insurmountable barrier, but thanks to cultural pluralism—or better, cultural relativism—the possibilities for choice have been doubled and can be expressed not in two ways but four: male heterosexual, female heterosexual, male homosexual, and female homosexual. Indeed, thanks to scientific progress, yet another possibility, bisexuality, has been added. A confused identity that excludes nothing is proposed as the most satisfactory, though it turns out to be least.

In this way of thinking, nothing counts as an obstacle to forming a family, so that homosexual couples—"de facto couples"—are also entitled to adopt children. Yet someone who understands identity as filiation, intimately related to origin, can ask how the children will develop their identity within a group that, although called a family, is not open to basic and radical sexual diversity. From the perspective of identity as affiliation or identification, there is no problem—all options remain open. Communities can be constructed at will, and the maximum openness is found in bisexual couples.

This approach takes for granted individual growth and development of a self-referential sort and closed to living with others. The individual is isolated within his self-affirmation. Such people can become politically correct citizens, duly socialized according to permissive values and standards. It appears less likely that they will be oriented toward social interaction, open to universality in joyful affirmation of diversity and complementarity.

The denial of living-with as a radical constituent of the person is a real possibility, not just theoretical or notional. It occurs through rejection of the original and transcendental receiving and giving of the person. The family is not only the basic cell of society. In the first place it is where the person originates and because of that it is the source of his personal identity. Within it one can learn in a natural way the essence of living with others—something that requires the simultaneous affirmation of unity and diversity—and the development of personal identity is grounded in this mutual openness. This form of identity and no other is necessary today to face the challenges of socialization and globalization.

Some apologies for the so-called traditional family lack anthropological weight, because they tend to remain discussions of sociological aspects—for example, the loss of social cohesion—found in other family "models." Or else they dwell on psychological aspects like the problem of an unbalanced development in infancy. The resulting arguments may be valid, but they are insufficient in the current situation, limited as it is by cultural and ethical relativism. It is necessary to go deeper into the human condition, for the surface, though real enough, does not encompass the whole reality of the human being. Analyzing isolated features in detail, we are at risk of missing the whole person and chattering about minutiae instead.

CHAPTER 3

"FAMILIES" AND THE FAMILY

(Alfredo Rodríguez)

1. THE QUESTION OF METHODOLOGY

In dealing with the family the first question to consider concerns the reasons, arguments, and methodology underlying statements in the vast literature on this subject. There are no good anthropological or ethical reasons to be seen, but perhaps sociology can find grounds for constructing models and types that will help us understand these formulations.

Family studies indicate that the evolution of the family in the West has involved three fundamental changes: a transition from the family as unit of production to unit of consumption; reduction in the number of family members and the concurrent disappearance of patriarchy; and a transition from extended family to nuclear family along with the diversification of family types.[1] One consequence of these changes has been that we now speak of families instead of family.

At present, then, "family" does not refer to the stable and permanent union of two persons of different sexes joined by a contractual bond and the purpose of procreation. This is just

---

1. M. Suares, *Mediando en sistemas familiares* (Barcelona: Paidós, 2002): 204–220.

one possible family type. Others include single-parent families, homosexual unions, and other de facto unions. As types of family, they are thought of as having the stability and permanence of the nuclear family. From this sociological perspective, the family can hardly be considered a unique social reality.

In this sense, Palacios says the concept of family has changed qualitatively, so that we can no longer speak of the family but of families.[2] Attention is focused on processes, functions, and values of the family types, not on the reasons for changes.

Studies like these exhibit no interest in what constitutes the core reality of the family and its nature. They concentrate instead on "intangible aspects" like goals, intimacy, projects, and shared ends.[3] Goals and lifestyles are more important than the make-up of the family, inasmuch as each family type involves a structure, an internal hierarchy, and rules governing relationships among the members and with the world outside.[4] To know these rules is the basis for understanding the new configuration of the family and designing any intervention in it.[5]

More could be said, but this is enough for present purposes. The intention of this chapter is to concentrate on sociological considerations in the attempt to explain what a family is—even though the family is prior to society and requires anthropological and ethical analysis. Here we shall consider the reduction of "family" to social types, beginning with the theoretical origins of this procedure, then considering how those abstractions are constructed, and finally examining whether this

2. Cf. M. J. Rodrigo, J. Palacios, eds., *Familia y desarrollo humano* (Madrid: Alianza, 1998).

3. Ibid.

4. Cf. L. Von Bertalanffy, *Perspectivas en la teoría general de sistemas: estudios científicos-filosóficos* (Madrid: Alianza, 1979). See also T. Parsons and R. F. Bales, *Family Socialization and Interaction Process* (New York: Free Press, 1955).

5. Cf. A. Gimeno, *La familia: el desafío de la diversidad* (Barcelona: Ariel, 1999).

is the best way to fully understand what families are and how they come to be.

2. THE SOCIAL AS THE SUPREME CATEGORY

The sociological approach to different forms of families has its origin in Comte. "Social" is the supreme category for him, where all the others acquire meaning and concreteness. It is expressed in the social solidarity of "humanity." It is important to bear in mind that Comte was active in an era of grave crisis, in respect to the anthropological question, so that it was left to sociology to attempt an answer to the crucial query: What is man? Flowing from this, obviously, is everything else. That pertains to humankind, for example: What is the family?

We find, then, a theoretical context extending to our time according to which the meaning of social activity is determined by society itself prior to the consideration of every social question. Everything—actions, relationships, modes of relating—is legitimate if socially "constructed." Sociological discourse then is at ease in accepting all diverse forms of relationships, without reference to the natures of the individuals who enter into them.

Zubiri remarks that humanity is the supreme reality in Comte's positivist vision, much as God has been for theology and even for metaphysics. Positivism inaugurates a new form of religion, "the religion of Humanity." Its supreme reality is not transcendent; it is the historical moment, immanent in society, with the physical universe as "theater" for the performance of humanity. In the end, social ideas and progress via relativistic process are the great motors and supreme forms of knowledge upon which foresight and provision for the future depend. This "provision" aims at what is best for each one on the way to the full realization of humanity. "Positivist philosophy is, then, the rational basis of human wisdom."[6] Here, in positivism and scientism, are the bases of methodological procedures in the social sciences.

It was Comte's intention that philosophy—public reasoning—be the supreme form of universal wisdom. In this way, according to Zubiri, "philosophy is nothing more than the rational form of a general condition of the human spirit . . . social or public reason of a positivistic character."[7]

Comte wishes to establish positivist philosophy as the organizing principle of social life, and for that he must show that it is the only possible solution to the historical crisis of his time, and the only basis for morality.

To show that it is the only answer to the crisis of his times, he proceeds in three stages. Ultimately, it is necessary for positivism to bring all social phenomena under its control.

To show that it is the only basis for morality, positivism invokes social sentiment as the basis of altruism and benevolence that generates solidarity among peoples. Man is no longer simply a person, but an individual existing in social solidarity. The moral subject now is *we*. The morality generated by social sentiment has bonds as strong as those of personal relationships. History will purify and systematize it. Positivism offers a new perspective to modern man by its way of understanding society and its problems.

Comte supplies the basis for moral relativism. He also establishes the foundations for the future development of collective conscience, and the body of doctrine that directs sociological reasoning. Its influence in sociological research is clear in the second generation of sociologists—Durkheim, Weber, Pareto—while it also provides the basis supporting social research in modern sociology. In summary, Ferrarotti notes the following contributions of Comte to sociological theory:

---

6. X. Zubiri, *Cinco lecciones de filosofía* (Madrid: Alianza Editorial, 2002): 148–149.
7. Ibid., 144.

- The fundamental interconnection of social phenomena, studied as the basis of sociological explanation.

- The positivist criterion, a fundamental presupposition of empirical research, which, though guided by theory, takes objective data derived by research as the supreme standard of what is true.[8]

Let us stop on this perspective of positivism for modern man, in the understanding of society. The sociologism found in the sociological discourse acquires the form of collective conscience in the formulation and explanation of multiple social phenomena.

Durkheim is an example of this. His understanding will introduce us into one of the keys of the current ideas about the family, and, in concrete, in the consideration of the different family models.

3. SOCIOLOGICAL KEY FOR SOCIAL UNDERSTANDING

Comte's ideas are important for understanding multiple social phenomena. Durkheim takes Comte's positivism and develops it in his sociological reasoning.[9] He seeks to provide sociology with a protocol that will allow a total and ultimate explanation of the social reality in which individuals must act. This is the necessary framework for making the individual a social being.[10] Thus we must agree with Tiryakian that "sociologism is more identified

---

8. F. Ferrarotti, *El pensamiento sociológico: de Augusto Comte a Marx Horkheimer* (Barcelona: Península, 1975): 277.

9. For a wider consideration of the relationship of Durkheim and Comte, see F. Múgica, *Emile Durkheim. Civilización y división del trabajo (II). La naturaleza moral del vínculo social* (Pamplona: Cuaderno Anuario Filosófico, 2004) n. 12.

10. "The man that education must form within us, is not such as nature has created him but such as nature wants him to be." E. Durkheim (1903). "*Pédagogie et sociologie*" in *Revue de Métaphysique et de Morale*, (11), 37–54, reproduced in *Educación y Sociología* (Barcelona: Península, 1996): 104.

with Durkheim than with any other author, though as far as I know, the term and its definition do not appear in his writings."[11] Durkheim's positive atheism and radical sociologism are clear when he states that "prior to the establishment of the sciences, religion played the same role, inasmuch as every mythology is a highly elaborated representation of man and the universe. In addition, science is the heir of religion (positive atheism). And religion is precisely a social institution (radical sociologism)."[12]

The foundation on which Durkheim's sociologism rests consists of three ideas.

a) *Social facts are a reality* sui generis, *different from the purely individual.* This is clearest in relation to collective conscience, a notion derived from the general will of Rousseau and the concept of consensus in Comte. Its suppositions are not exclusively cognitive. Durkheim moves beyond his predecessors most significantly in dealing with solidarity and with it, presumably, collective conscience not just as givens, but as variables. From this arises the distinction between organic and mechanical solidarity. The collective conscience is understood, then, as the collection of beliefs and feelings shared by typical members of a society. It is not a Platonic idea, but something with its own reality—an entity—although it may not take material form. According to Durkheim, the continued existence of society depends on it.[13]

b) *The relationship of the individual to society.* Durkheim assigns primacy to society over the individual: The individual arises from society, not society from individuals.

11. E. Tiryakian, *Sociologismo y existencialismo. Dos enfoques sobre el individuo y la sociedad* (Buenos Aires: Amorrortu Editores, 1962): 25.

12. E. Durkheim, *Educación y Sociología*, (1996): 59. The parentheses are added.

13. Cf. E. Durkheim, *De la division du travail social*, 4ᵗʰ ed. (París: P.U.F. 1996): 46.

Numerous texts by Durkheim make this point, e.g., "The product par excellence of collective activity is that collection of intellectual and moral goods that we call civilization . . . . Civilization makes man. It is civilization that distinguishes him from the animal. Man is only man insofar as he is civil."[14]

c) *The priority of the whole over the parts.* Durkheim observes that the social whole cannot be reduced to the sum of its elements and so cannot be explained by them. Individual phenomena reflect the condition of the collective, not vice-versa. It follows that to explain social differentiation one cannot start from individual conscience, since individual conscience "is a simple, subordinated form of the collective type and follows all its movements, in the same way as an object, property of an individual, follows those of its owner."[15] Every explanation of social reality must be grounded in the collective conscience. In this way, a social fact can only have a social cause.

Durkheim writes: "Individualistic sociology does no more than simply apply to social life the principle of the old materialistic metaphysics. In fact, it attempts to explain what is complex by the simple, the superior by the inferior, the whole by the part, which is contradictory in itself. True, the contrary principle does not seem more sustainable. It is not possible to derive the part from the whole, as the idealistic and theological metaphysics pretends, given that the whole is nothing without the parts that compose it and cannot draw from nothing that which it needs to exist. Thus, it is only possible to explain phenomena found in the whole on the basis of the characteristic properties

---

14. E. Durkheim, "*L'évolution pédagogique en France, Vol. II: De la Renaissance à nos jours*" in *Educación como socialización* (Salamanca: Sígueme, 1976): 37.

15. E. Durkheim, *De la division du travail social*, 100.

of the whole, what is complex from the complex, social facts from society, vital and mental facts from the *sui generis* combinations from which they derive."[16] While Durkheim emphasizes the superiority of the collective over the individual, he does not demonstrate it empirically. The underlying assumption is simply that what is more complex is superior to what is less complex. Nevertheless, the idea has powerfully influenced the literature of sociology and is pervasive in sociological discourse concerning the family. It is in the background of talk about family models—particular modes of collective conscience—where it offers support to individual autonomy and ever-expanding areas of freedom that permit everyone to opt for whatever "model" he prefers.

This is so because the superiority of the collective over the individual pertains not only to functionality but to morals, insofar as morals are "a social function, or better, a system of functions that was developed and consolidated little by little through the pressure of collective needs."[17] The functional character of morality, according to Durkheim, does not empty morality of its contents nor take away the role of the individual as social protagonist. To act morally, it is necessary that, "either obeying a rule or dedicating ourselves to a collective ideal, we have full and clear awareness of the reasons for our conduct. Because it is this awareness that gives our action the autonomy required . . . of any truly and fully moral being."[18]

16. E. Durkheim, "*Epresentaciones individuales y representaciones colectivas*" in *Revue de Métaphysique et de Morale*, VI (1898): 273–302, taken from *Educación como socialización*, 77–78.

17. E. Durkheim, "*La science positive de la morale en Allemagne*," in *Revue Philosophique*, XXIV, (1887), 46, quoted by E. Tiryakian, *Sociologismo y existencialismo*, 44.

18. E. Durkheim, *L'Education morale*, prólogo de P. Fauconnet (París: Alcan, 1925): 136–137. Translation of Everret K. Wilson and Herman Schnurer, *Moral Education: A Study in the Theory and Application of the Sociology of Education*, with foreword of Everret K. Wilson (New York: Free Press of Glencoe, 1961): 120. There is a Spanish translation, *La educación moral* (Buenos Aires: Shcapire, 1972): 135–136.

Here is one of the key principles of current talk about the family: the imperative that I be recognized as socially distinct from the others. It is not a matter of explaining who or what I am. The only certainty is that I am not like the rest. This is how sociologism achieves its supposed synthesis between individual and society, with the latter retaining its primacy yet leaving some room for individualism and autonomy. Morality has a key role in all this. Durkheim says: "Insofar as societies have increased in size, the bond uniting men among themselves has stopped being personal."[19] Moral relationships are established in progressively more universal, and therefore more egalitarian, terms, filling in the gaps that used to separate individuals and classes.[20] Individual autonomy, attached to collective conscience, finds in morality a more abstract type of bonding, replacing the one that formerly existed between persons. This bonding is as powerful as the community in which it exists.

The social—Comte's supreme category—finds in the collective conscience of Durkheim the way in which social phenomena are expressed concretely. For morality, what is conventional replaces what is natural.

In considering this important key to understanding sociological talk about the family, we need to address something else: the formation and foundation of ideal types of behavior. This second key will allow us to understand how constructivism becomes influential for its account of the development of diverse social phenomena. From a different perspective than Durkheim, Weber looks more to the origin of the social milieu and the possibility of modifying it through behavior. The only cause of human action is the decision of the actor. Nevertheless,

19. E. Durkheim, *"La science positive de la morale en Allemagne,"* Revue Philosophique, XXIV (1898): 123. Quoted by F. Múgica, *Civilización y división del trabajo (II)*, 46.

20. Ibid.

as we will see, Weber's account is more a product of deduction—behavioral models drawn from theoretical knowledge—than it is of deliberation. In this way the person as such disappears from view.

4. THE FORMATION OF IDEAL TYPES

The cognitivist perspective of Weber's ideal types for the understanding of social reality has hermeneutics as its foundation, given that the ideal type is a useful fiction that does not exist as such in reality. Weber expresses this when he says that "every interpretation seeks evidence. But no interpretation of meaning . . . can pretend . . . to be also a valid causal interpretation. In itself, it is nothing more than a causal hypothesis which is particularly evident."[21]

The reason is to be found in what Max Weber understands by ideal types: "They are images in which we construe relationships . . . that our imagination, formed and oriented according to reality, considers adequate."[22]

The ideal type is, then, a concept by which we try to explain the essential features of a frequently occurring phenomenon; it is "the window through which we interpret and know reality."[23]

How Weber's ideal types function is stated in other words by Aron, who says: "The construction of the ideal types is an expression of the effort that all scientific disciplines make to impose intelligibility on matter, deducing from it an internal rationality, and perhaps even constructing this rationality . . . . Finally, the ideal type is related also to the analytic and partial conception of causality. In fact, it allows us to apprehend

---

21. M. Weber, *Economía y Sociedad. Esbozo de una sociología comprensiva* (México: Fondo de cultura económica, 1984).

22. M. Weber, *Essais sur la théorie de la science, traduit de l'allemand et introduit par Julien Freund* (París: Plon, 1965): 185.

23. A. Rodríguez, C. Parra, F. Altarejos, *Pensar la sociedad. Una iniciación a la sociología*, 2th ed. (Pamplona: EUNSA, 2003): 97.

historical individuals. But it is a partial apprehension of a larger whole."[24]

Thus considered, the ideal types of Weber give rise to the problem of meaning, the question is not what reality is, but what it means for me. Hermeneutics in this way has a strong relativist and historicist coloration. According to this view, truth is a historical phenomenon determined within a particular context in light of a "global vision of cultural values," in Weber's phrase. But the idea of historical context is itself a mix of factors arbitrarily selected. This is precisely the task that Weber assigns to the social sciences.[25]

The analysis of behavior by the methods of research requires the identification of values and their relationship to choice. In human action, a calculus of values is indispensable to making decisions. But choice also brings to light irreducibility of values and the conflict among them. There is here no guarantee of unconditional validity in reference to human action; choice is always necessary. For Weber, this means recognizing one's situation prior to choosing and then consistently choosing the value or values that best suit the situation. Suitability, according to Weber, is determined by criteria implicit in the methodology of identifying values.

Consistent with the complexity of this interpretative system, there is a certain indeterminacy regarding the truth. Hermeneutical expositions are frequently obscure and contain numerous variables. If there is no definitive truth, it will surely not be found in hermeneutics, although it can bring us somewhat closer to truth.

Weber proposes to lead us closer to truth via ideal types, along a path leading from simple realities to complex ones, while

---

24. R. Aron, *Las etapas del pensamiento sociológico. Durkheim-Pareto-Weber* (Buenos Aires: Siglo Veinte, 1992): 262.

25. Cf. M. Weber, *Ensayos sobre metodología sociológica* (Buenos Aires: Amorrortu, 1982).

at the same time complex phenomena are broken down into simple ones. The approach is necessarily analytic and deductive.

5. FOUNDATIONS OF IDEAL TYPES

Two conditions serve as foundations for the construction of the ideal types:

1) There are to be no prior assumptions about value questions.
2) Science must verify its assertions by its own causal explanations.

Analysis of these two conditions and their possible realization constitutes the guiding lines of Weber's methodology. This analysis is found first in the essay "*Cognitive Objectivity of Social Science and Social Policy,*" and later in "*Critical Studies on the Logic of Science and Culture.*"

The study of the first principle takes up the distinction between value judgment and value relationship. The desired goal of objectivity in research rules out making value judgments. Scientific research focuses on what is, not what ought to be. "An empirical science cannot teach anybody what must be done, but only what he can do and, under some circumstances, what he wants."[26] In this way, a distinction, familiar to the social sciences, is drawn between judgments of fact and judgments of value. The approach is of course strongly relativistic.

The identification of value is no more than a choice, inasmuch as the criteria that determine the result of choice amid a multiplicity of data are neither universal nor necessary,[27] but themselves are products of choice. Weber states:

---

26. M. Weber, "*La objetividad cognoscitiva de la ciencia social y de la política social,*" in *Ensayos sobre metodología sociológica*, 44.

27. "It is impossible to conclude in a univocal manner obligatory cultural contents, and certainly so much less the more inclusive may be the contents in question," Ibid., 46.

"Drawing a decision from that weighing is not among the appropriate tasks of science. It is proper to man and his will: weighing the values involved, he chooses among them according to his own sense of things and his personal vision of the world. Science can make one aware that every action implies taking a position in favor of some particular values and, as a rule, against others. But choosing is, in practice, up to the individual."[28]

It is characteristic of Weber's method that choice extends not only to empirical data but also to the criteria by which values are identified. The identification of values indicates the emphasis behind an investigation. Still, Weber aspires to find a theoretical conceptual framework that will be valid in all times and places—bearing in mind the variations that historical developments place before scientific research.[29]

The analysis of the second condition is determined by the way in which the first is understood. Given that an explanation is restricted to a limited series of factors, determined in each case by a particular point of view, there is also a choice to be made. The question is what cause-effect relationships clearly explain the phenomenon. The solution involves constructing a hypothetical process that excludes one or several elements and comparing this with what are known to be matters of fact. Based on its explanatory power, this allows one to attribute more or less causal importance to the construct.

Comparing the hypothetical process and the real one allows one to establish the causal importance of this element in relation to the phenomenon to be explained. Not all causes are examined, however, but only those relevant to the predetermined focus of the research. In this way, Weber's methodology

---

28. Ibid., 42.

29. "In fact, it is and will continue being true that a scientific demonstration which is correct in its methodology, within the social sciences, if it pretends to have reached its goal, has to be recognized as correct by a Chinese, also," Ibid., 47.

abandons the classical method of investigating causality, in favor of a conditional one.

For Weber, the central task of this method is to reduce complex phenomena to simple ones. Weber places the accent on analysis and deduction rather than deliberation. The perception of social reality via the ideal types is a methodological solution to the complexity of social reality. We turn next to how this methodological procedure brings us to an understanding of society.

6. IDEAL TYPES AND SOCIAL UNDERSTANDING

Weber attempts to unify two concepts—understanding and explanation—as essential elements of the sociology he tries to elaborate. His *Economía y Sociedad*[30] embodies this effort. The starting point is to show that social action is the behavior examined by sociology. The meaning of a behavior sheds light on a social relationship.

Comprehensive sociology is centered on the elaboration of ideal types of behavior, forms of social action that can be discerned in the behavior of the individuals. The "specific object" of comprehensive sociology is neither an internal state nor external behavior, but action; and this always means "behavior understandable in relation to objects, that is, a behavior specified by the sense (subjective) inherent in it or attributed to it."[31] To see how Weber understands the proper task of sociology, let us look at his understanding of society.

Weber distinguishes clearly two aspects of social action: an internal one, constituting the field of intentionality and meaning,

---

30. Cf. M. Weber, *Economía y Sociedad* (México: Fondo de Cultura Económica, 1944).

31. M. Weber, *"Sobre algunas categorías de la sociología comprensiva,"* in *Ensayos sobre metodología sociológica*, 177.

and an external one, in which a causal process is translated into human behavior. In light of this distinction, there are three decisive terms to keep in mind: comprehension (*verstehen*), in other words, the way we learn the meanings of social action; interpretation (*deuten*), the possibility of organizing the subjective sense in concepts; and explanation (*elklären*), that is, the way in which causal processes become visible in the recurrence of patterns of social conduct.[32] The fundamental point of Weber's methodology, as Sahay points out, is that sociological analysis operates by means of values, individuality, and comprehension; while the four forms of ideal type are different means of relating these methodological principles, each depends on a particular type.[33] Weber's procedure consists of the following steps.

- First, clarifying the inherent value of the process of action by the meaning or sense of the action being analyzed. The meaning may be personal, psychological, social, or historical, as will be shown by the interpretation given to the action by the actor or the participant.

- Second, constructing a typical-ideal norm of comparison, with which the given interpretation is compared in order to attribute a cause to the correlated facts of the interpretation.

- Third, generalizing from such individual causal attributions.

- Finally, and logically, a process of abstraction that allows one to make conditional predictions concerning social change.

This procedure is key to understanding the framework in which social sciences will develop.

---

32. R. Aron, *Las etapas del pensamiento sociológico*, 286.

33. Cf. A. Sahay, "*La importancia de la metodología de Weber en la explicación sociológica*," in *Max Weber y la sociología moderna* (Buenos Aires: Piados, 1974).

The importance of Weber's comprehensive sociology resides not only in his developing a new methodology; nor in showing how diverse sciences are interrelated; nor in giving an autonomous character to the diverse social sciences. Weber's exposition involves a rupture between reflection on method and a theory of values. It does not deny values, but it does deny them scientific consideration. In consequence of the negation of their unconditional character, values cannot be treated scientifically. Weber confronts a problem with no easy answer: how one should relate to values, understood as a world view, once they have lost their absolute character. What is the significance of values understood as chosen rather than given?

First of all, for Weber "values are not found in what is sensible or in the transcendent. They are created by human decisions different in nature from those by which he apprehends reality, and works out what is true. It is possible that, as some neo-Kantian philosophers have said, truth itself may be a value. But in Max Weber there is a fundamental difference between the order of science and the order of values. The essence of the first is the subjection of consciousness to facts and proofs, while the essence of the second lies in free decision and free affirmation. Nobody can be forced by a rational proof to recognize a value that he does not accept."[34]

To accomplish this task, Weber again considers the distinction between objective investigation by the historico-social sciences and value judgments. His solution is very similar to that in his essay *La objetividad cognoscitiva de la ciencia social y de la política social*. Nevertheless, the problem he considers has larger meaning: do the historico-social sciences have anything to say regarding values? For Weber, historico-social sciences cannot render an opinion about the normative validity of values, but they can establish empirically their existence and clarify the conditions

34. R. Aron, *Las etapas del pensamiento sociológico*, 269.

and consequences of their realization. Technical criticism of values can establish the proportionality of means to ends, and the relationship of this with the other consequences. Thus Weber does not reject empirical criticism of values. Such criticism does not concern goals but means, that is, the conditions that conduce to the realization of a value taken as an end. He does not prejudge the validity of this or that value, but establishes that some means are more appropriate than others to attaining certain ends and the realization of certain values. In this way, Weber shows that a choice among a multiplicity of values determines the point of view from which research will be carried on.

By assigning a contingent character to values, as Weber does, the necessary relationship between transcendent values, systematically structured and human action, which is compelled to recognize the absolute character of such values, is replaced by a relationship between normative criteria capable of being realized and human action whose validity is determined by the choice it carries out.

This makes it clear that one's view of values is decided by a choice. "The problem of the choice of values brings us to the ethics of conviction (*Gesinnungsethik*). Moral conviction calls upon each of us to act according to his or her feelings, with no implicit or explicit reference to consequences."[35]

In the case of the historico-social sciences, the adoption of certain values through a choice based on a value judgment established the criteria of the research and limits the field of action to be examined. In the case of natural sciences, whose logical structure excludes value relationships, the individual is aware of the relationship between means and goals intrinsic to a process of technical elaboration, i.e., the accomplishment of a desired goal. In the case of human action, which

---

35. Ibid., 274.

assumes values, certain values are upheld in preference to others, either from an ethic of responsibility or from an ethic of conviction.

7. SOME CONSIDERATIONS ON THE QUESTION OF TYPES

Despite Weber's genius, there is a difficulty involved in this procedure. Although generalization involving ideal types are very helpful to the comprehension of numerous social phenomena, it is no less true that the reductionism involved in this process of generalizing fails to recognize the individuality of the various types of person. That each person may be a type—in relation to profession, age, sex, origin, etc.—and that relationships can be established between types, do not exclude the fact that a person cannot be reduced to a type. Nor is a person the sum of types discernible in his performing a function, being of a particular sex and age group, or coming from a particular geographical place. Contrary to Weber's approach, we must conclude that a person is irreducible to types, inasmuch as he can transcend these and continue growing. Where the family is concerned, this is of great importance. The family is an instance of an environment that evolves according to the individual types that compose it; but the members that constitute it are not reduced to those types and the family embraces the individualities of all.

That the family itself is not a type means that the functionalist discourse is not the most adequate way of understanding its reality. The functionality within the family is not excluded, but it is not taken as the starting point. This, however, is what generally happens in sociological discourse on the family that considers it exclusively from society's point of view. That sociology may contribute a great deal to understanding the family is undoubtedly true. But there is no doubt, too, that consideration of the family from society's perspective impoverishes and distorts the proper nature of the family. On what grounds then are we to affirm that the family is the basic cell of society? A widely studied example will suffice: unemployment. Can government allow a rate of unemployment of 20%, as happened some years ago in Spain, if the family is not there to provide support? Any expert on the matter will realize that without the family, the institutional breakdown of the government will occur. But something similar occurs with the productivity of a country. If everybody devotes himself to work and there is no family institution to back this up, could we reach the standard of productivity that is demanded? Undoubtedly not. Society does not solve the problems that the family addresses. It follows that it only makes sense for the government, even out of self-interest, to protect the family as the basic cell of society, quite apart from any functional consideration. This is the lesson of countries where the family has not been protected, and a collapse has ended in social disintegration.

Considering what we have just discussed, it appears that a concept of person in a general sense—as proposed by the authors mentioned—is insufficient, because the personal being in its ultimate nature is open to the universal, not to the general.[36] And what environment accepts this openness to the universal better than the family? It would be better to say that society imitates, insofar as it can, coexistence in the family, and takes from it numerous beneficial aspects. Such at least is the attitude that seems to be present in numerous new social phenomena. What happens with immigration? To consider a person as an immigrant is to characterize him or her in a general sense. What is the attitude of the government and, more so, of the populace toward this new situation? It might be to consider that an immigrant is, above all, a person who can become

---

36. The distinction between the general and the universal has been explained in Chapter II, Section 4.

destereotyped by becoming a citizen of the country that has received him.

Ending the stereotyping of persons culturally enriches a nation's people. We are not trying to establish a new collective conscience, but to give priority to the person over his stereotype. The reality of the family exceeds the collective conscience, and the solidarity existing beyond this destereotyping is the opposite to a collective conscience which is supported by the principle of nondiscrimination; then, in the family a person's filiation takes precedence over his affiliation. Obviously this can create problems for the organization of a society, but its problematical nature demands that we approach these in the indicated direction. Families from Peru, Ecuador, Morroco, and Spain have it in common—*unum*—that they are family, while their diversity—*in diversis*—lies in geographical and cultural origin, which facilitates social dialogue and the development of a society.

Without this consideration of types, social consistency turns out to be problematical because it is basically an ethical problem and exclusively human.[37] The reason why it is exclusively human is based on the fact that "the personal being is not determined by his biological species, nor exhausted by it, because there are so many additional persons of the same species."[38] The exclusively human problem "is based on his relationship with his peers."[39]

Why is this relationship with peers a problem? Precisely by the "recognition of the personal character of the others . . . because effectively that is what happens to a person who does not exhaust his species: he finds himself coexisting with other

37. L. Polo, *Ética. Hacia una versión moderna de los temas clásicos* (Madrid: Unión Editorial, 1996): 72 and 78.

38. F. Múgica, "*Introducción,*" in L. Polo, *Sobre la existencia cristiana* (Pamplona: EUNSA, 1996): 45.

39. Ibid.

persons of the same species . . . and given that we are not final-ized by it, we are in a communicative relationship with others who also have it, which is human society."[40] Why is the act of recognition problematical? Because it is a matter of realizing that "the social problem has to do with the consideration of the other as neighbor."[41] And this is crucial to understanding the family and family relationships.

The social problem becomes more acute when the diverse stereotypes lead us to feel that the neighbor—the immigrant mentioned earlier—is not as much of a person as ourselves. This is possible by the "objectivation" involved—in the sense pro-posed by Max Weber—and, consequently, the reduction of the person by a partial recognition, determined by the typification. An example can illustrate what we are saying: "Man is *sapiens*. If someone deals with another as if he were not, that is, does not recognize his character as a person, he reduces him to *habilis*, to an animal. Slavery is a purely instrumental way of dealing with a human being, based on the negation of his char-acter as a person."[42]

Appealing to the notion of neighbor reinforces social and family consistency, avoiding any type of reductionism which would bring with it the objectivation of types. This reinforce-ment through the notion of neighbor is only possible through interior dispositions which permit a person to recognize as neighbor any of his fellow men. And this disposition originates from virtues.

But then, these interior dispositions make us realize that the understanding of society is possible only from ethics, and not, as Weber says, from a "cultural world vision of values" that involves relativism. Thus, ethics appears as the "fundamental

---

40. L. Polo, *Ética*, 73.
41. Ibid., 78.
42. Ibid., 79.

condition"[43] of social consistency. This condition, as opposed to Weber, emphasizes the anti-objectivist character of a systemic compression of society.

8. SOCIAL TYPES AND THE FAMILY

"If we consider the individual as a subject or a person (person is nothing more than the transcendental amplification of subject), the constitution of the family is intrinsically complex, and has to be approached as such in its study."[44] And that is precisely the objective of the types: to begin considering human complexity.

Nevertheless, as we already noted, Weber's proposal involves a reduction of the human types to social types. Such a reduction results precisely from the generalizing character of social types, which do not take into account all the aspects or dimensions of the individual type. "For that reason, the organizational social solutions, based on the notion of type, exactly because they are general, do not attain agreement between the human types taken in their more proper sense, given that each human being is a type."[45] And we would have to add that it is not reduced to the type it represents, but transcends it.

The generalization of types, from an exclusively sociological perspective, runs the risk of denaturalizing social organizations, precisely in its attempts to find in the type the solution to the diverse forms of organization. In those solutions diversity becomes subsumed in the generality, by the complexity involved in confronting the relationships established when we notice that in each person we find a series of dimensions of an individual type, in other words, each person is a type.

---

43. L. Polo, *Quién es el hombre: un espíritu en el tiempo* (Madrid: Rialp, 2003): 126.

44. F. Altarejos, M. Matínez, M. R. Buxarrais, and A. Bernal, *Familia, valores y educación* (Santiago: Seminario Interuniversitario de Teoría de la Educación, 2004): 11.

45. L. Polo, *Conocimiento del hombre desde una epagogé sistémica: los tipos humanos* (unpublished manuscript): 5.

With respect to the family, the generalization of types involves, more and more often, adopting a social and juridical form that results in the loss of the first distinction between types: being a man or a woman. The assimilation of one to the other supposes a "massification," a generalization which is proper to social types, because it makes no sense to want to belong to a different type when a person belongs to one. Behind this intention lies the issue of the replacement of nature by culture, a thing much more easily manageable by the methodology involved in the construction of diverse types, as has been shown.

In this way we obtain the simplicity sought by the types, when the criterion of unity is the model, not the person, with the risk noted by Morin: "Let us take man as an example. Man is evidently a biological being. He is at the same time a cultural being, meta-biologic, and lives in a universe of ideas, of conscience, and of language. But in regard to those two realities, the biological and the cultural, the paradigm of simplification forces us either to their decoupling, or to reducing the more complex to the less complex."[46]

To be a man or a woman corresponds to a typological difference that goes much further than being individuals of the same species: to be male or female. Types as ways of expression derive from and correspond to the person, although the types correspond to a lower level than that of personal character. When people decide to get married, they do not propose to marry a female or a male, but Jane or John Doe, insofar as they are persons, and recognizing the typological difference favors such union. Noting that the union goes beyond their being individuals of the same species, it is recognized precisely in the stable and permanent character which is desired for such union, as opposed to what we can observe among animals, who do not

---

46. E. Morin, *Introducción al pensamiento complejo* (Barcelona: Gedisa, 1997): 89.

go beyond the threshold of species and whose union takes place precisely insofar as they are male and female. Even when there is typological diversity among animals, such diversity does not go beyond the threshold of the species to which they belong. The absence of personal character confers on that typological difference a more determinist character in its action. This absence of a personal character prevents members of the animal species from being or wanting to be of a different type than they are.

We should not forget that types, seen from the perspective of the person, are modes of manifestation. And in this way: "man is not manifested in a uniform way, but is manifested according to types, and the manifestation of the types is above all personal, so that to generalize is to lose one's typical character."[47] To say about somebody that she or he is a woman or a man, and no more, is a generalization. What one is, is a masculine or feminine person. The feminine or the masculine does not exhaust the type, because each woman has features that are hers and hers only, which make her different from any other woman, as happens also in the case of a man. Nor does each man or each woman exhaust masculinity or femininity. To keep in mind this consideration is a key to the diverse modes of manifestation of a man or a woman. This diversity—being a woman or a man—through its connection with personal character, is precisely what enriches and gives sense to family coexistence, and at the same time enriches social coexistence.

From a logical perspective, the typological diversity that we are referring to has to do with a type of opposition, which often we are not aware of. We are referring to the relative opposition in which we distinguish, intellectually and really, the extremes; it is not less true that both are mutually complementary.[48]

---

47. L. Polo, *Conocimiento del hombre*, 5.
48. Cf. J. J. Sanguineti, *Lógica*, 5th ed. (Pamplona: EUNSA, 2000): 79–81.

Although clearly opposed, to be a woman or to be a man, they are not in conflict because of that, given their mutual necessity and interdependence. This intimate interdependence of the types cannot be appreciated in social typology given its generalizing character. To demand that sociology consider within its typology the diverse types of individuals is to go beyond its proper method, as has been shown. Only when these types are connected with personal character, can we really advance in our comprehension of typology and the enrichment that human manifestations involve in the social milieu.

There is no doubt that the diverse types and the relationships to which they give rise have undergone changes over time. Certainly abuses have occurred; and greater knowledge of the human being has allowed us to get beyond some typologies that impoverish persons and society. A clear example is slavery. This was for centuries a socially permitted typology. One can conceive of persons who are free and others who are slaves. The primacy of human dignity and the linkage of types to personal character make it possible to see here a social construct unrelated to the reality of the person.

Something similar has occurred in the treatment of women in the family. If the person is reduced to a type, consideration of the family is reduced to a mere functional exposition. Function seemed fixed in accord with the type represented and the family relationship that was established. This led, among other things, to understanding the family institution as a clan, rather than considering the family as a central and nuclear institution. "The woman, first of all, belongs to one clan, and the man to another. Clans tend to avoid marriage within the group, a kind of prohibition of incest. When the typical organization is the clan, incest is understood as ruling out not only marriage between brothers and sisters or cousins but also within the clan. Marriage then is a relationship outside the clan: women of one clan marry men from another. But membership in a clan can be stronger than the institution of the family, so that when a family breaks down, the woman returns to being a member of her original clan. The family in this case is what is often called an extended family."[49]

On the other side, the institution of the family, considered as a nucleus, destroys that idea of clan, which only remains as an abstraction. In the perspective from which we are considering the family—the types—the institution of the family is a coordination of male and female according to individuality. The monogamous family is the one that is best suited to the human types, because they are "his" and "her" types who bind themselves together, not social types according to clan. The family relationship is a relation of human types with their own individualities, not merely a sexual relationship. To be human is to be able to enter into the loving relationship of giving and receiving; and that requires the cooperation of persons, not members of a clan. In this way the family constitutes a new cell which, supported by the individuality of each, contributes in the best possible manner to the humanization of the social types.

In the institution of the family lies the key to coordination in respect for one's own type and that of the other. But then there is no room for generalization, as we have seen in the proposal of Weber. The richness of the family institution consists precisely in taking into account all the aspects of the type or all the dimensions of the individual type.

9. CONCLUSION

Social coexistence is channeled according to diverse formalities, the types. If effectively society is the channel and connection of the diverse types, it cannot be avoided. In this sense, human

---

49. L. Polo, *Conocimiento del hombre*, 6.

action exists as social action or else it does not exist. In this way, for Weber social action is identified with the types.

This gives us a clue to an important question: the social problem becomes more acute when the diverse typifications lead us to suppose that our neighbor is not as much a person as ourselves. This is possible by the objectivization involved in the typifications and then the reduction of the person to a partial recognition, based on typification.

This objectivist perspective hampers the analysis of personal relationships within the family, which will be the theme of another chapter. To give primacy to the person and to understand that the action is not self-grounded eases the consideration of the diverse types and the relationships among them—given the anti-objectivist character of the family and of society—opening up the possibility of understanding the family as an environment for personal growth, and of improving social consistency through the family.

CHAPTER 4

EDUCATIONAL FRAMEWORK OF PERSONAL RELATIONSHIPS

(Aurora Bernal, Martínez de Soria)

1. THE BIOGRAPHIES

Most biographies start the same way: "So and so was born here or there in such a year. He was the second of so many children, his father had this profession and his mother's name was . . . " To some extent, we know someone if we know his family. Similarly, the study of the human being by anthropology ends up dealing with the subject of the family, as we have seen in the preceding chapters.

Philosophy for a long time devoted itself to the subject of man. But later this split off as the discipline of anthropology, whose focus shifts between what the human being is, can be, and ought to be. Anyone who thinks seriously about the human being quickly notes his special value, especially when observing those human actions that go beyond subsistence. This same thing happens to the singular and concrete *homo sapiens* if he is not overwhelmed by the need simply to conserve his life.

The discovery of human dignity requires us to show what reveals his reality. The categories of person, freedom, love, identity, and coexistence express the reality of what we are and what we hope to become until we reach excellence, which in terms of human life is usually called happiness. These "abstract" notions are real if they correspond to human life. Focusing on the family, with these anthropological categories, supplies a framework to understand not only its logical or conceptual existence but its real being. In the family we can understand, from experience and from theoretical reflection, what it means to be a person, what freedom consists in, how we love, how we recognize identity, how we experience coexistence.

The quality of this understanding rests upon the answer to two simultaneous questions: the what and the how of the personal being—what it is to be a person and how this is gradually revealed. This is why well-written biographies do not ignore the subject's family roots. The discovery of the personal, denominated in different ways, in its dynamic dimension—realization, development, growth, evolution—is an educational process. Family education is the kind of instruction involved in the mild threat: "life will teach you." But to understand human dignity, and the properties that reveal the special value of the human being, according to which we call him a person, we go to the family in whose womb those particular beings come to be.

To meet those who are and belong in the family, and to know how these persons and no others act, today raises a slippery problem: what exactly is a family? In the prior chapters we have confronted this problem. The issue of the types of families clouds the study of family reality more than it clarifies it. The idea of family models irritates many people, because it is either a forced imposition or a utopia. Notwithstanding, from the perspective of what it seems reasonable to say about the person and his development, we have to say something about what the family is, to be able to show some educational content.

While some experts question whether we can define basic principles of social and family organization, others state that there is more than enough proof of the differences associated with growing up in this or that family environment, of having family stability, of having to learn to coexist or living in a continuous conflict.[1] Studies on the subject are multiplying.[2] And at the tip of the confusion we find some professionals—family counselors or therapists—who claim that we have to define what the family is, contrary to the opinion of numerous specialists in family theory. We have reached the point of relativizing the family by attempting to encompass today's large variety of organizations and coexistences that bear some resemblance to the family; and this leaves the counselors perplexed and uncertain as to who require their services.[3] In the broader arenas of law, politics, and economy, we find similar confusion.

From a reasonable position based on human dignity, we shall attempt in the following pages to see what the family is, as a basis for considering how those making it up should be raised. Taking into account the large number of studies whose data show the crisis of the family and the failure of the family to integrate or to form persons, we feel that this does not invalidate the reasonableness of our proposal. For example, a farmer may note that wheat, once sown, will grow if there is rain. But some years bring drought lasting for months. We don't ask ourselves: should the wheat grow in such conditions? It has not rained, so we decide to water it. Similarly, therapists attempt to provide remedies to recover or supplement interpersonal relationships that have been lost in a crisis or family breakdown.

2. AUTHENTIC FRAMEWORK OF HUMAN RELATIONSHIPS

The human sciences that deal with the family are characterized by constant and basic discussion of personal relationships. In this

---

1. Cf. M. J. Palacios, *Familia y desarrollo humano* (Madrid: Alianza, 1989): 39.

2. Cf. D. H. Demo, M. J. Cox, "Families with Young Children: A Review of Research in the 1990s," *Journal of Marriage and Family*, 62 (2000): 879–880.

3. Cf. A. R. Wiley, A. Ebata, "Reaching American Families: Making Diversity Real in Family Life Education," *Family Relations*, 53 (2004): 273.

case, application of the interdisciplinary principle means centering attention on relationships among persons who are members
of the same family. Whether coming from the theoretical human
sciences or from the theory of practical sciences, authors deal in
the why and how of the setting of interpersonal relationships. As
has been said, we observe the domination of sociology in the way
its formulas on the framework of family relationships extend into
other sciences. We encounter expressions of family classification
such as cell or basic unit of society, space, institution, system, and
scenario. Social or socio-cultural anthropology is also steeped in
this way of looking at the reality of the family, although at the
beginning it adds to the social prism the variations proper to different peoples, noting the predominance of the nuclear family.[4]

Family may be a society, a space, or a scenario for the relationship of a group of persons; but we must say something
more precise to distinguish it from other societies, other fields,
other scenarios. The key to emphasizing its specific note lies in
distinguishing those that relate and why. This is what gives
sense to the other characteristics usually invoked when some
precision is sought about what the family is, such as: coexistence in space and time, in a home and for a long period, sharing intimacy, which attains an affective and rational dimension
with the establishment of some degree of commitment to permanence. This is the hard question that needs to be elucidated,
to avoid falling into sterile distinctions or confusion of the issue.

Prior to studying the singular aspect of family relationships,
it seems useful to remark on the option adopted out of all the
sociological categories that could have been chosen to point
out the place of family relationships. The notion closest to what
we attempt to discuss in this chapter is environment, from
which we could derive the concept of scenario or "stage," a
term currently fashionable. To talk about "scenario" seems

---

4. Cf. C. P. Kottak, *Espejo para la humanidad. Introducción a la Antropología cultura*, 3ʳᵈ ed. (Madrid: McGraw-Hill, 2003): 104.

more attractive to us because we are able to represent better what we want to say. On the stage, actors play roles; in the family, members perform functions. Indeed, they perform a number of them, as we have said. Among all of those roles, the educative function stands out, a special characterization of the family "stage," because the family is an environment.

The environment is a space, considered in an analogical sense because it lacks physical dimensions. It is "constituted by relationships between persons, which we know through representations and which have the consistency determined by the attitudes that the individuals maintain among themselves, the institutional norms, and the goals which, in a more or less permanent way, are being sought."[5]

In its internal dimension, the environment is translated into a "we," an encounter between persons. The term "encounter" is reminiscent of the anthropology of some authors of the twentieth century, which has been taken over from some pedagogical currents that mention it as a crucial element in the development of the human being as a person.[6] Persons relate to things and show their genuine being especially when they create and transform. The human being is shown in a positive light when he takes advantage of the possibility of contributing something new and valuable. This relation of a person with reality that opens up for him the possibility of creation gives shape to an environment. Realities which are sources of possibilities receive the name environments.[7]

5. Cf. E. Martín López, *Familia y sociedad. Una introducción a la sociología de la familia* (Madrid: Rialp, 2000): 46.

6. One of the most commonly mentioned authors, in this sense, is Martin Buber, and especially his work "I and Thou," cf. M. Buber, *Yo y tú* (Madrid: Caparrós, 1993). The ideas of the relevance of the other, the meeting, recognition, and existential communication are present in numerous authors: Jaspers, Marcel, Levinas, etc.

7. Cf. A. López Quintás, *El secreto de una vida lograda: curso de pedagogía del amor y la familia* (Madrid: Palabra, 2003): 41–70, based on Buber's anthropology, defines that sense of environment.

Persons develop environments if they seek each other and are realized in their meeting. In mutual discovery, persons reciprocally discern their possibilities, among which stand out those of creating relationships of coexistence, worthy modes of vital unity because they allow each person to give his best. For the human being to expand to his full potential, it is necessary to elevate concrete and singular reality into an environment. This tends to start in the family. Due to its elemental characteristics, environments can be configured into environment (as in sociology) or environments (as in anthropology) if the relationships between the members are directed toward and promote the possibilities of the others. The family is an anthropological reality—a relational one—required by the constitution of the human being, who is also a relational being.

It can be stated without presumption that there is a consensus over the interest and the protagonist role of personal relationships in the family, and their importance for the welfare of persons. There is also a consensus on the repercussions of this form of life on social dynamics in all its aspects: economic, political, civic, etc. The first meaning of the word family is the relationship of persons due to kinship, which determines some form of common life. It is a transcultural phenomenon, as evident as the succession of generations.

2.1. Relationships between the sexes and between generations

The nexus between family and kinship, due to conjugality and procreation, can serve to speak about families in numerous analogous senses, with reference to what happens when we study relationships marked by consanguinity. Kinship supposes a bond by consanguinity, affinity, adoption, marriage, or some other stable analogous relationship. One can see that semantics involves a practical goal—mutual understanding— and facilitates evident concerns, which at least serve as starting points although they may not exhaust the meaning.

The debate over what the word kinship means continues among social anthropologists. The discussion has led to the claim—perhaps from academic exhaustion—that this category should be replaced by relationality. This polemic reminds us of another, no less heated: That concerning the connection between nature and culture, between what we think is fixed and what is variable. The reference of one controversy to the other is seen most clearly in the attempt to replace the sense of kinship as a fixed structure of relationship by the sense of kinship as process.[8]

Consanguinity refers to the generative relationship between two persons, a man and a woman, which results in the birth of other persons, who in their turn are related. Without this reference, discussion of what the family is, is meaningless. This bond is what gives meaning to talk about other family relationships: children, grandparents, uncles, cousins, etc. Among all the family relationships, that of being a son or daughter is the most basic. From there a relationship is established between each person and his siblings, grandparents, uncles, and aunts.

This consideration does not exclude the fact that often in ordinary life grandparents may affirm their grandchildren more than their parents or that a brother may be the main point of reference for some person. In other situations, we say accurately enough that such and such a grandfather has been like a father. "One plays the role of . . . " also in the case of adoption. Such references refer to the natural way human generation takes place, a condition sufficient to distinguish the existence of a family.

The bond between generations is vital and universal. The kinship bond is characteristic of all persons. The genetic heredity involved serves as substratum to begin to see that each

---

8. Cf. L. Stone, *Kinship and Family: An Anthropological Reader* (London: Blackwell, 2004): 1–23.

human being is unique. The context in which such singularity is found allows us to seek out what is personal in the human being. There could be a group of persons by reason of kinship who collaborate mutually in the satisfaction of biological necessities, in the same way animal species do. The comparison with animals brings out the cultural contribution of the human species, given that other type of necessities are satisfied, those that contribute to humanization. Our immaturity at birth is only solved through the care of the progenitors during a long period of time, leading to common life.

The peculiarity of such care is the interaction which develops the spiritual dimension of the human being. For this reason, the family is qualified as the original reality within which the specifically human emerges.[9] That this care is instinctive becomes hidden, which is the reason why human beings develop rules for that way of life and the regulating of those relationships. The natural bonds are not established solely by reason of biology nor are they limited to the satisfaction of biological needs, but they open up to psychic and spiritual content, to modes of feeling and self-perception, to ways of knowing and of knowing ourselves, to ways of loving and of self-love. Family relationships are open so widely that they encompass all dimensions of human existence.

2.2. Consistency of relationships

There is evidence that the naturalness of the family must not be measured only by biological criteria in the variety of forms of established families. The mode of family relationships is chosen, and because of this choice, respectable. Nevertheless, what we can observe in any situation is that choice is no guarantee of high quality in what has been chosen. This can be applied to

---

9. We have left aside the discussion over the issue of what was first: society or social group, or the family. This issue occupies pages and pages of social or political philosophy and social anthropology.

family relationships. We have to see which relationships favor the person and which do not. This analysis places the reflection, as we have indicated in the first chapter, in the field of philosophical anthropology. The main question is to understand what there is, or what is done in the family, so that the human being may be recognized as a person. This capacity of recognition differentiates the human being from the animal. From there derives the oft-repeated statement that the family is a place of humanization.

Not all families promote relationships with the same validity. Some even seem to be trying to break them. We can understand the reaction of some authors in view of the loss of credibility of the family pejoratively called traditional: "Even the so-called normal family may not be the place where we find a universal and long-lasting fondness. In general we see clearly in it the presence of belonging and mutual co-responsibility."[10] It does not seem so important to see what functions are realized by the family, but the problem that preoccupies us the most in practice is why the family assumes those functions.

What makes the family different from a mere aggregate of human beings joined for reasons of subsistence is revealed by the fact that other goals are sought in that bonding. We become united so that each one can live—so that each has a good life or can *live well*. In fact, those goals do not exclude each other. One refers to subsistence, the other to welfare, and the third includes higher goals, above all love. Love involves a spectrum of human phenomena, arising from intimacy, and it ranges from pleasure in qualities that satisfy us to the gift of self and the acceptance of a person for what he or she is.

Family relationships involve subjects that can affirm one another for who they are and not for the way they behave, although in the flux of rationality behavior can have consequences.

---

10. Cf. E. Beck-Gernsheim, *La reinvención de la familia: en busca de nuevas formas de convivencia* (Barcelona: Paidós, 2003): 75.

This principle operates between spouses, from parents to children, children toward their parents, siblings among themselves, grandparents and grandchildren, uncles, nephews, cousins, etc. The possible affirmations of some to the others are multiplied according to family membership. They are established with greater or lesser intensity depending on numerous factors that delimit the fundamental question about mutual affirmation between human beings: to choose to love the other and do our best to promote his or her integral goods. This choice and its permanence are what we call love.

Within the family environment the roots of the person develop. It is a place of coexistence where it is possible and natural—proper to human nature—to love, to accept the existence of other persons and contribute to their potentialities. One's own freedom is elevated—the greatest degree of freedom is to be capable of giving oneself—and this is done to promote the freedom of the other. Reciprocity and gratuity are understood. Mutual dependence of persons is lived, which is the basis of belonging. From this dependence a properly understood independence arises, and becomes compatible with social life: "The recognition of dependence is the key to independence."[11] The "personal" bond does not limit action but is a source of personal actions.

The family, in this sense, can be understood as community. Each member transcends his ego and makes it "we." Each goes beyond himself when he enters into communion with another: as wife, as husband, as father, as mother, as son, as daughter. From this communion of one "I" and another "I," we pass to a community. The I is found in the we in a fuller way, as a person. The person, seeking the common good, not only does not lose his own, but is confirmed as a person. The "we" is defined by the bonds of belonging, so

---

11. A. MacIntyre, *Animales racionales y dependientes. Por qué los seres humanos necesitamos las virtudes* (Barcelona: Paidós, 2001): 103.

that conditions must be created in order that each one can be himself. It is as important to attain this good for everyone as to collaborate in getting it by coexisting. The members of a family are transcended in the family and the family is transcended in society. The path from multi-subjectivity to the subjectivity of the many is the true meaning of the *we*.[12] That "we" has its origin in the family. It is worth examining the depth of family relationships.

3. PATERNITY AND MATERNITY

Conjugality is the beginning of the family. In the conjugal relationship two intimately related issues are in play: being spouses and being parents. In both cases one person is recognized and accepted as unique and different in relation to another: the other spouse and the child. The conjugal relationship presupposes acceptance and recognition of the other as someone of a different sex—equal as person, unique as himself or herself. Only a man can be father of this child, only a woman can be mother. The gratuitous reciprocity between persons of different sexes is the reciprocity of two full persons.[13] This is confirmed in generation, although it is not reduced to that.

Reciprocity between the sexes is the foundation of the value of values, the greatest value of human dignity: life. "Human paternity constitutes man in a new way, by making him a father of a new human being."[14] The same is accomplished through maternity. The exercise of paternity leads to a growth of the qualities of the man as father; the fact long recognized and

12. Cf. K. Wojtyla, *El hombre y su destino. Ensayos de Antropología* (Madrid: Rialp, 1998): 98.

13. Cf. B. Castilla Cortázar, *Persona y género: ser varón y ser mujer* (Barcelona: Ediciones Internacionales Universitarias, 1997).

14. Cf. L. Polo, *Ética. Hacia una versión moderna de los temas clásicos* (Madrid: Union Editorial, 1996): 65.

appreciated about the maternity of the woman is now starting to be recognized with similar force about the man.[15] A child is born already "related" to his parents, and for this reason he wants to know who they are, even in painful situations. The affirmation of the other in the conjugal relationship renders possible the acceptance of another person's life. The person is constitutionally *dialogical*, open to other persons, in his sexual character and in his origin. Some authors have defined the human individual as a familial being. The reciprocity of the sexes leads to the reciprocity of the generations. Or in more pragmatic and utilitarian terms, deduced from an empirical sociology: "Without a contract between the sexes there will be no contract between generations. The future of the inter-generational contract will depend on attaining a new configuration of the relationship between the sexes."[16] These are the source of many and much. Paternity and maternity continues in the education of the children. Although in some cultures this responsibility has been entrusted mainly to the mother, it can now be shown that, even for merely utilitarian reasons, both father and mother need to be intensely involved in the care and education of their children.[17]

The entry of women into the labor market makes it more necessary for father and mother to share the work of caring for children. Lack of time, among other factors, moves the parents to tend to the most immediate needs of their children, while perhaps delegating further elements of their education to educational institutions. In educational centers, teachers expect parents to take part in the education of their children, in addition

---

15. Cf. R. Frank, *The Involved Father: Family-Tested Solutions for Getting Dads to Participate More in the Daily Lives of Their Children* (New York: St. Martin's Press, 1999): 185–163.

16. Cf. E. Beck-Gernsheim, *La reinvención de la familia*, 160–161.

17. Cf. D. Méda, *El tiempo de las mujeres. Conciliación entre vida familiar y profesional entre hombres y mujeres* (Madrid: Narcea, 2002).

to providing for their welfare, so that it is mandatory that the father and mother become involved. Due to the widely recognized changes in the labor and demographic fields, it seems necessary for the family to change, with great effort and imagination, so that it will remain the primary community of love and solidarity.

This educational innovation of greater parental cooperation in the education of their children, though imposed by circumstances, has some advantages. Father and mother will be enriched by educating their children in a process arising from their procreative role; and the education also is enriched, in that more teachers means higher quality. The subject of paternity has been neglected, compared to the numerous studies of maternity. It is not enough to analyze the greater or lesser abandonment of the family by the father—a matter of concern, even in the political sphere—the degree of activity of the father must also be considered.[18] Studies have shown that there is a role for the father in early infancy as well, and that his activity is not merely complementary to the mother's.[19]

The investigation of paternity uncovers familial educational styles, organized according to the exercise of authority. To this one must add other issues that have come to light relating to aspects of sexual identity. Numerous investigators emphasize the role played by male and female influences in forming the personality of the child.[20] One could amplify this analysis by more deeply understanding the nature of gender identity. A

---

18. Cf. S. Coltrane, "The Paradox of Fatherhood: Predicting the Future of Men's Family Involvement," in W. D. Allen, L. Eiklenborg, eds., *Vision 2003: Contemporary Family Issues* (Minneapolis, MN: National Council of Family Relations, 2003).

19. Cf. A. Polaino, *Familia y autoestima* (Barcelona: Ariel, 2003): 97–99.

20 Cf. Kyle D. Pruett, *Fatherneed: Why Father Care Is As Essential As Mother Care for Your Child* (New York: Free Press, 2000); C. Jenkins, S. McHale, A. Crouter, "Dimensions of Mothers and Fathers – Differential Treatment of Siblings: Links with Adolescents' Sex-Typed Personal Qualities," in *Family Relations*, 52 (2002): 82–89.

person by being man or woman possesses a series of aptitudes, attitudes, and potential qualities intrinsically related to other qualities attributed to him or her as a unique person. Living together with different people has great educational potential. In addition, in the family environment we find a duality of persons—father and mother—to which is added the duality of gender. This personal meaning has its roots in love—the first civilizing step in overcoming instinct—because it affirms the other for who he or she is, someone who is accepted and who acts, deploying all his or her potentialities, in this case, as father or mother.

In the context of personal development (which is not the building of an identity starting from zero and which cannot ignore who this person already is) that facet is revealed in which each one assumes his or her own gender as a function of the relationship established with another. We are dealing with a duality of relationship. It often thought that the success of marriage is based on finding numerous points in common, with a minimum of differences, "but the conjugal union is not based on increasing equality until a uniform identity between two is achieved. It is based precisely on the proper grasp of two great human diversities, being a man and being a woman."[21]

3.1. Predominance of affectivity

Although we find attempts to understand the relationship between genders with no reference to conjugality, this logically continues to shape what it means to be of one gender or the other. Today there is a special difficulty in getting to know persons of the other gender, because sexuality has been reduced to sex[22] and sex to functionality, to criteria of usefulness, although it may be disguised as pleasant affection. We no longer talk only

---

21. Cf. J. L. Viladrich, *El ser conyugal* (Madrid: Rialp, 2001): 53.
22. Cf. J. Marías, *Mapa del mundo personal* (Madrid: Alianza, 1994).

about sex or gender but about sexual orientation, which indicates that these distinctions, made for purposes of identity, are more properly being seen as matters of choice or of identification. The personal area of life is bound within the wide margins established with effort in love, which leads one to be willing to share one's life as a whole, and not only psycho-physical traits. The result of reducing an interpersonal relationship to usefulness, even if a high one, is to disregard persons and attribute to gender a distinct new meaning. With reference to this, it is illuminating to see the different social attitudes, analyzed sociologically, as a consequence of the differentiation of persons by their sex. This can be examined in the family and also as it is projected in society.[23] The relationship can be that of coexistence (in a different sense than that discussed in the second section, it refers to using the other as an object); or it can be one of self-interest—the exchange of useful favors; or of life together, with reciprocity of life, affection, communication; or of community, including a plan of life, openness to procreation, with a sense of permanence, of service, of full self-giving. In the family we find community relationships, if they are the ones that rule conjugal life. To form a community, not just a group, better suits the personal way of being.

In order to carry out this experience of community, it is necessary to distinguish love from feeling—a project of shared life to develop the person from a network of affection and welfare. The first provides stability, the second continuous variability. Often the family is seen as a kind of affective refuge, fed by all the possible relationships, including the paternal. Parents sometimes seek satisfaction from their children by seeing in them their own prolongation. The support provided by affection is shown in opinion polls to be the function of the family

---

23. Cf. E. Martín López, *Familia y sociedad*, 31–45.

most appreciated, in the eyes of many parents and children.[24] Even in attempts to define the type of community of the family, understanding the relationships of reciprocal affirmation among the members who integrate what is plural, love is only considered in its affective dimension of feeling good with the other or making the other feel good.[25]

Psychology has abundant descriptions of the affective dynamic of individuals and interpersonal relationships. The result is a constant insistence on the affective climate. To a degree this is logical, because what is observed with greater ease are the emotions and feelings of a person. But the affective dimension correlates with the moral dimension and the use of freedom. The person grows if he integrates everything that he is into his behavior. To promote this, we have to think what the family should be like. It has to have a plan, goals—among which values are paramount. In light of these values, means are chosen, and these are partial ends. The interpersonal relationships in the family provide opportunities of growth for its members. If there are no ends, or they are limited to an environment of emotional balance, the framework of the family is weakened until it is lost. The constant effort toward self-giving of its members "is reduced to a mere association of mutual aid."[26]

This situation can be foreseen in such obvious signs as lack of a common task and of communication. But if the effort of self-giving is present, the family will welcome whatever is always radically new in history, that is, the person. To accept in this way requires continuous learning by all the family members. Inside the family, persons are more likely to be valued. Valuation is an intrinsic element of love, and it is the bond of

---

24. Cf. P. Pérez Alonso-Geta, ed., *Valores y pautas de interacción familiar en la adolescencia (13–18 años)* (Madrid: Fundación Santa María, 2002): 194–195.

25. Cf. T. Neira, "*Pedagogía y educación familiar,*" in E. Castillo, eds., *Educación familiar : nuevas relaciones humanas y humanizadoras* (Madrid: Narcea, 2002): 19.

26. Cf. F. D'Agostino, *Elementos para una filosofía de la familia* (Madrid: Rialp, 1991): 17.

relationship.[27] The exercise of love involves a way of using freedom, which includes everything that the person is. It affects especially the integration of affectivity in its rational, intellectual, and volitional dimensions, thus obtaining the best result. It is understandable that the family constitutes an excellent place where, together with the development of affectivity, moral education can find a place in daily life.[28]

4. BEING SONS AND DAUGHTERS

To call oneself son is equivalent to defining one's identity by one's origin. The son, by being who he is, deserves an origin commensurate with his personal dignity. As a matter of fact, paternal-filial relationships can originate in a generation in a variety of circumstances, even unworthy ones. This possibility does not negate the fact that relationships between human beings take on the personal character of those involved. This is demanded from the perspective of their being, and for this reason they are owed it. As we realize, following the line of thought of the prior explanations, what is personal is better guaranteed if paternity and maternity are entered into in a life project of reciprocal giving, found best in the family.

The dignity of the person does not depend on the circumstances of his begetting, or the quality of his parents. In theory, no one is any greater than another by being the child of this or that person; at most, one may have more than another. But each one, in his own self-esteem, is affected by the knowledge of who his parents are. Each person learns to know himself by recognizing himself in the others, starting with his parents. It is quite fitting that one's parents become the first points of reference.

---

27. Cf. L. Polo, *Quien es el hombre*, 79.

28. Cf. J. E. Grusec, L. Kuczynski, *Parenting and Children's Internalization of Values: A Handbook of Contemporary Theory* (New York: John Wiley & Sons, 1997).

The sense of belonging is important from the psychological, sociological, and moral perspectives. We recognize what we are from infancy because our perceptions about ourselves coincide to a large extent with the perceptions of the others: "It is possible to state that a person knows who he is in reality and that he is, only because there are other persons of whom it can be said that they really know who and what that person is."[29]

People take confidence from knowing that their origin was in a context of love and they were wanted by their parents, but also from knowing that they are something more than their parents' desire. That legitimates their personal nature and their freedom.

It gives confidence to know that one is the fruit of love and its acceptance by one's parents. A child needs from his parents recognition, security, and constant companionship, and to be accepted for who he is, the child, not loved in proportion to his qualities. In other words, each person has gained something important in his life when he knows about his origin, and this origin corresponds to the mutual donation of a man and a woman, open to the acceptance of whoever proceeds from their love. In their love, they love the one to whom they give life, not for having "produced" him.

Having reached this point, we encounter the mystery of life—a mystery for those who, without science, always believed there was something sacred in human origins, and a mystery for those who, with science, discover there is a great leap from what is described by biology to what occurs in human begetting. It is astonishing how the genetic makeup of each person is configured, requiring the coming together of their parents and the parents of their parents, stretching all the way back to the earliest generations.

---

29. Cf. A. MacIntyre, *Animales racionales y dependientes*, 113.

Each person is the culmination of a set of unrepeatable and unique circumstances that determine him as this particular being and not someone else. And a greater mystery is recognized when the fruit of this process is not a more or less variable individual within the homogeneity of a species, but a person whose existence transcends the existence of a group of biological factors, converging in an apparently contingent form; elements necessary for the existence of a new human being, but not enough to explain the human freedom proper to each person and to each of his progenitors and ancestry throughout history. For those who may not have been wanted by their parents, there is always the possibility of being accepted by other people and by the Origin of all origins, as is explained in those religions in which creation by God, concurring in the procreative act of the parents, is fundamental to the account of human nature.

The gift in the origin of a person, who is accepted in everything that he is and can become, configures the continuous donation involved in maternity and paternity during the life of the protagonists. To receive it is also a vital project which always supposes acts of love, although they may appear as mere nurturing. If we admit human dignity in its deepest sense, the subject of its origin is not irrelevant in theory or in practice. If we accept the dignity of the person, we cannot reduce his origin to a natural determination of the biological order.

The child expresses towards his parents the relationship of origin; and recognizing his parents, he begins to recognize who he is. That, as has been explained above, says something important about personal identity. The person is characterized, also, by recognizing himself as *who he is*, and not just how he is. The first question relating to *who one is* is that of origin. The relationship turns out to be reciprocal, which means a child will always have a debt to his parents and will owe them love throughout his life. This recognition stimulates the ethical talents of people from within. Since antiquity, the relationship between origin and duty has been understood as the virtue of piety.

Each one asks himself: Do I owe something to someone, do I originate from someone? "Individuals attain their own good only insofar as others make of that good their own good, helping during times of incapacity, so that in time they will turn . . . into the kind of human beings who make the good of others their own good."[30] Knowing one's origin makes it easier to choose the end, to behave freely and not merely independently. Without that origin, man becomes centered on himself, without roots, and this lack of roots, as we know, produces people who do not fit well into society and tend not to have families.[31] Someone who has a good father will himself aspire to be a good father. Trust leads to the hope—the virtue and passion—necessary to formulate a plan for one's life.

The child perceives who he or she is through the affection of parents. This is the educational resource that has the greatest impact. Care shows love and produces trust, and it is the necessary setting for the exercise of authority, which leads a person to orient his affectivity according to someone else's will until he is able to do it by himself. Psychological research into attachment, and its consequences in the development of self-esteem and the concept of self, reinforce this feature.[32] When a climate of acceptance, of care, of affection is established, children from early infancy observe and imitate their parents, and compare themselves with them; they interiorize that experience, and the behavior they imitate serves them as an indicator of personal identity. The value they attribute to their parents serves as

---

30. Ibid., 128–129.

31. Cf. L. Polo, *Quién es*, 152.

32. Cf. J. Alonso García, J. M. Román Sánchez, *Educación familiar y autoconcepto en niños pequeños* (Madrid: Pirámide, 2003).

criterion for their own self-esteem.[33] In that climate of protection they subject to the test everything that they experience, they acquire a sense of reality, and through these family relationships, they begin to value their own practical judgments, distancing themselves from immediate desires, thanks to their parents' authority.

For this development, the stability of the union of the parents is a clear advantage. That union is usually strengthened by marriage. The expression "figure of stable attachment" is used in psychology to describe the effect on children of a permanent link to those who care for them. In some nations with a long tradition of divorce—in the sense that it has become a custom—social policies have been adapted that aim at promoting marriage, with laws that protect it better[34] and with educational programs to prevent divorce.[35] After considerable social experimentation, it is generally agreed that cohabitation involves a clear risk that there will be no marriage or the marriage will end in divorce. It appears that the children of divorced parents have a tendency to end their marriages as soon as difficulty appears.[36] Despite some accusations that

33. Cf. A. Polaino, *Familia y autoestima*, 33ff. The well-regarded attitudes of parents for the development of self-esteem in their children are: unconditional, total and permanent acceptance of the children, independent of their way of being; constant, realistic, and stable affection; involvement of the parents with each child's person, circumstances, needs, etc. Personal consistency of the parents, educational style (clear expectations and limits); objective valuation of the behavior of each child, motivating, praising efforts and accomplishments, and correcting errors provide trust and security.

34. Cf. S. Skolnick, "Uncle Sam, Matchmaker: Marriage as a Public Policy," in W. D. Allen, L. Eiklenborg, eds., *Vision 2003: Contemporary Family Issues* (Minneapolis, MN: National Council on Family Relations, 2003): 11–15.

35. Cf. H. J. Markman, S. M. Stanley, G. H. Kline, "Why Marriage Education Can Work and How Government Can Be Involved: Illustrations from the PREP (the Prevention and Relationship Enhancement Program) Approach," in W. D. Allen, L. Eiklensborg, eds., *Vision 2003: Contemporary Family Issues*, 16–26.

36. Cf. P. R. Amato, D. Deboer, "The Transmission of Marital Instability Across Generations: Relationship Skills or Commitment to Marriage?" *Journal of Marriage and Family*, 63 (2001): 1038–1051.

those who carry out this research are conservative authors, the ideological arguments fail when the facts are examined: the harmful impact of divorce on children, wife and husband, varying according to differing family situations.[37] Marital conflict and divorce damage the emotional stability of the children and have consequences in their familial and social behavior.[38] Poor results in school have also been shown. A great deal of the work of family counselors is trying to solve the difficulties that arise after a divorce.[39]

To be a child is more fundamental than to be a parent, since one is always a child. To recognize oneself as child is to recognize one's dependence—that one has not decided to exist or not, has not chosen who one is, has not chosen one's parents. This recognition brings one into touch with a reality that provides many keys for the development of what one is. It has also a significant ethical background, a necessary foundation for learning values. The child grows: to do that is owed to his parents towards whom he is not independent, though he does have to grow in freedom. To accept this is the beginning of sociability. Accepting one's dependence on others, one grows more.

The person, recognizing himself as child of his parents, accepts his siblings and grandparents, with whom he has a unique bond. The relationship between brothers and sisters develops as a friendship that educationally and sociologically propels each toward social life. Brothers and sisters are not chosen, and therefore maintaining a bond facilitated by being of

---

37. Cf. J. Walker, "Radiating Messages: An International Perspective," *Family Relations*, 52 (2003): 406–417.

38. Cf. P. R. Amato, A. Booth, *A Generation at Risk: Growing Up in an Era of Family Upheaval* (Cambridge, MA: Harvard University, 1997); E. M. Hetherington, J. Kelly, *For Better or For Worse: Divorce Reconsidered* (New York: W.W. Norton & Company, Inc., 2002).

39. Cf. K. Leon, "Risk and Protective Factors in Young Children Adjustment to Parental Divorce: A Review of the Research," *Family Relations*, 52 (2003): 258–270.

the same family, forming a relationship of almost near-equals, requires a greater effort of self-giving between them, since they obviously owe each other less. Learning such gratuity is a source of sociability that helps make societies more personal. What happens with children who belong to families where the relationships are different is being studied. This refers to families where the parents do not live together, children have other tutors, perhaps other brothers and sisters, and lose contact with their grandparents.[40]

5. THE FAMILY AS EDUCATOR

Education flows from the vital core of personal relationships established in the familial community. Relationships educate as long as they persist, and they can be an environment of permanent education. In the family, one can always observe education or its absence; it is not a neutral factor with respect to the formation of persons. Relationships develop together with the simultaneous order and disorder of human life, combining contingency (what befalls the family from the outside and could have been different) and freedom (which gives rise to the contingent and permits the acceptance of what is necessary). Reality cannot simply be organized to teach lessons. The family in itself is a school of living, and "produces" education through the lived relationships of the members. How these relationships are established—limited by the freedom of the protagonists—determines education. If family relationships are based on love, they always empower the other, and this building up is of the essence of educational activity. In the last chapter we shall analyze the form of that particular education. Now we can remark on three kinds of educational contents that can be deduced from this special human community. In one way or another,

---

40. Cf. E. Beck-Gernsheim, *La reinvención de la familia*, 77.

programs of education for the family reflect in general the following objectives and contents.[41]

a) One learns to act in freedom, to count on it, to expand it, to combine dependency with independence and responsibility; one learns affective control and the integration of affectivity, and its extension to the core of what constitutes love. One discovers freedom in the onerous yet fulfilling act of serving others. The family is a place of well being—it helps every member to be born, to grow, to find nourishment, to feel good—which is necessary so that the person will be at ease in other social areas, will acquire the qualities to make a living, fulfill his social function, and develop a new environment for a good life.

Note that the family is the place from which social capital arises.[42] So that this result may be possible, the family needs to become a theater of good living which, according to the Aristotelian idea, is what the actors of the family scene can attain. The advantages of family life ought to surpass its inconveniences. Interfamilial relationships should be established for reasons that go beyond the "good life" to a life that is truly good. One learns to rise above problems, to suffer with support, with strength, with unity.[43] One learns to be confident, to be certain. One makes a habit of all this with naturalness, in an environment that allows each one to be

41. Cf. L. H. Powell, *Family Life Education: An Introduction* (Mountainview, CA: Mayfield, 2001).

42. Cf. R. Crosnoe, "Social Capital and the Interplay of Families and Schools," *Journal of Marriage and Family*, 66 (2004): 267–280.

43. Cf. M. D. Glantz, J. L. Johnson, eds., *Resilience and Development: Positive Life Adaptations* (New York: Kluwer Academic/Plenum Publishers, 1999): 41; L. H. Ganong, M. Coleman, "Family Resilience in Multiple Contexts," *Journal of Marriage and Family*, 64 (2002): 346–348.

what he is, and learn, without external coercion, to be a better person.

b) One learns to be oneself; and this empowers one to grow with balance if one has the experience of being loved unconditionally. "Each human being can have deep personal roots and identifies himself as identifying with 'his own'—those with whom there is a co-belonging that is true and unconditional."[44] As an extension of learning one's identity, one learns to accept the diversity of persons. The practical exercise of this teaching is expressed in the fluid communication of someone willing to listen and to talk.

Among the possible diversities is one specific to the family, the diversity of sex. This duality of male and female is the origin of the family and of society. Within the family one can learn sexual identity, the diverse manners of reacting, of organizing one's life, of dealing with others. One learns equity, the importance of masculinity and femininity, the relevance of both of these to being a father or a mother, or to being companions in the case of brothers and sisters. One learns to be father and mother, although this may be described in research from a negative view, citing the bad experiences of sons or daughters to show how difficult it can be to be a good parent.[45] One learns the diversity of age, diversity of temperament, diversity in free acts. One learns to accept and to help a handicapped person, a vulnerable person, especially in dealing with children, the sick, and the elderly. Assuming

---

44. Cf. J. L. Vildarich, *El modelo antropológico del matrimonio* (Madrid: Rialp, 2001): 100.

45. Cf. D. Jacobovitz, "Fostering Resilience in Children: The Importance of Early Relationship Experiences," in W. D. Allen, L. Eiklenborg, eds., *Vision 2003: Contemporary Family Issues*, 53–58.

their acceptance as persons, these are not only tolerated but respected.

c) One learns to turn a society into a community. To
deal with the other as who he or she is involves a way
of acting, of performing functions with constancy due
to a commitment, that is learned by imitation. It constitutes a source of civilization. The family is the
matrix of individuals and of society; it may be the
mold of persons behaving as such, and in this sense
the family is the bosom of a personalized society.
Civilization consists in knowing how to transform the
unfamiliar into the familiar.[46]

The sociable dimension of the person expands as solidarity—contributing to a community of persons—and not only as
socialization, i.e., adaptation to a group and milieu. It originates
and is nourished in the family, primarily if this is understood and
lived as a life project in the terms already mentioned: recognition
and acceptance of who they are, accepting self-giving, self-giving
of diverse persons by sex, age, and freedom. The family becomes
a privileged environment of links between peoples, so fruitless
that it opens up to other persons in society and leads to altruism
and a culture of disinterested unity with others.

---

46. P. Donati, *Manual de Sociología de la familia* (Pamplona: EUNSA, 2003): 21.

CHAPTER 5

THE FAMILY ENVIRONMENT:
Trust and Respect

(Concepción Naval)

1. INTRODUCTION

In recent years we have witnessed growing interest in the family,[1] from various disciplines. The founding of interdisciplinary research institutes in several universities to promote these studies is an example of the concern this subject has evoked.

We can ask ourselves why we have lately once again become concerned with this subject, why we long for the family. Referring to citizenship education, F. Audigier, an educational theorist, says something that can be applied also to the family: we come back to it at times of crisis.[2] In fact, we are suffering now from a lack of sociability; individualism has damaged personal relationships, and we are suffering because of it.[3]

---

1. Cf. J. A. Myers-Walls, P. Somlai, eds., *Families as Educators for Global Citizenship* (Ashgate, VT: 2001); R. Colomina, "*Activitat conjunta i influencia educativa en el context familiar*" *Educar*, 28, (2001): 181-204; E. Beck-Gersheim, *La reinvención de la familia: en busca de nuevas formas de convivencia* (Barcelona: Paidós, 2003); J. Alonso, J. M. Román Sánchez, *Educación familiar y autoconcepto en niños pequeños* (Madrid: Pirámide, 2003).

2. F. Audigier, *Teaching About Society Passing on Values. Elementary Law in Civic Education. A Secondary Education for Europe* (Strasbourg: Council of Europe Publishing, 1996).

3. Note what was pointed out in Chapter I about the distinction between person and individual.

As a result, our sights turn back to the family as the natural place of personal relationships, where we can learn to live them out; here we learn to be persons, in relation to the next door neighbors, so that later on we can open up to others farther away. In addition to family relationships, the child receives also formation of his personality, of his sociability. The environment has influence, and can have some effect, but there is no question about the great weight that the family exerts.

In this chapter we shall refer to the family as the seedbed of society and of the development of natural sociability and show how the experience of family life helps in those areas, concretely, by providing an environment of trust and respect in family relationships.

2. FAMILIAR RELATIONSHIPS

The rediscovery of the important place of the family as an educational setting in the contemporary world has been associated with the criticism aimed at extreme liberalism from various angles. I refer to the communitarian critique and, to a certain extent, the feminist one.

The first looks to the family and small communities as opportunities to recover meaning and orientation in human relationships, in view of the care for and attention to members that is characteristic of them. The communitarian critique of liberalism[4] is multiple, having to do with political philosophy and the general concept of man and society.[5]

Communitarians denounce liberalism as lacking concern for intermediate communities, indispensable elements of human existence, to the point of letting them disappear. It

---

4. Cf. C. Naval, *Educar ciudadanos. La polémica liberal-comunitarista en educación*, 2ⁿᵈ ed. (Pamplona: EUNSA, 2000).

5. Cf. A. Buchanan, "Assessing Communitarian Critique of Liberalism," *Ethics*, 99 (1989): 852-882; S. Holmes, *The Anatomy of Antiliberalism* (Cambridge, MA: Harvard University Press, 1993).

devalues civil life, they say, by considering political society a mere instrumental good, without grasping that the participation of citizens in the political community is an important part of the good life. It fails to recognize certain obligations and commitments that are not the result of contracts—as, for example, family obligations, service to the country, or the priority of the common good over individual interests. It conveys an erroneous conception of the I, refusing to admit that it is always *located* in a socio-cultural and historic context, and is *constituted* at least in part, by values and commitments that are not matter of choice nor revocable at will. It causes an inflation of the policy of rights (claiming rights, seeking to maximize one's interests, without considering whether this is at the expense of the goods owed to others).[6] And in the end it ignores the central role of language, culture, customs, praxis, and shared values, as the bases of a true recognition of collective identities and rights.

The feminist critique of liberalism, among varied and controversial arguments, raises questions about the need to recover a more balanced vision, human and unitary, of the life of women and men, in which caring for self and others, and not only duties and responsibilities, is the proximate horizon of human relations.

2.1. Current research

It is a fact recognized in experience and documented by research that the kind of relationships established within the family decisively affect how the child sees and understands itself and learns how to act in society, behaving as a social being.[7]

---

6. Cf. M. J. Sandel, *Liberalism and its Crisis* (Oxford: Basil Blackwell, 1984): 31 and 183.

7. A subtle and ironical criticism of present-day familial relationships can be found in A. Digby, ed., *Full Circle? Bringing up Children in the Post-Permissive Society* (Exeter, G.B.: Crowley Esmonde Ltd., 1988).

Self-confidence is required, together with personal security, to adapt and open up to others. Knowing and feeling oneself to be "at home" helps realize the mission of the nuclear family, that of being "seedbed of society," the first place where a child learns to socialize and social virtues are formed.

Socialization is frequently understood as the acceptance of social values by the individual, that is, as incorporation of collective standards into one's way of feeling and thinking. In psychological terms, we speak of *internalization*. The term points graphically to the external meaning and extrinsic origin, from the outside to the inside of the subject, involved in socialization. No doubt we must speak of "social influences" in the development of the personality. Who can deny it? The open question is how such influence is realized. When socialization is employed according to the sense used here, influence means conformation or suitability of the subject to the feelings, convictions or ideas that socialize. In this way, education turns out to be the accommodation or adaptation of the subject to what has been taught, which raises the question: Could it be done some other way?

There is, however, another response arising from a way of thinking that runs from Rousseau to Dewey and has significantly different features but marked continuity. It views education as "development," thus implying that growth and maturation occur in the subject from the inside out. This vision corresponds to the consideration of the human being as a person, with all that it implies.[8] Here social values are indispensable points of reference, but also elements of contrast and of support for personal development. Socialization, then, does not consist of adaptation to something external, but of collective assistance to the growth of the person. Society is as necessary to man as water to fishes, but only as an environment,

---

8. See Chapter 4.

not as a forge on which personality is hammered out and citizens produced according to the ideals of society. And the family is, no doubt, the primary environment that leads to personal growth. Looked at from a complementary perspective, observing the behavior of the child or adolescent on the social stage, we might intuit in some way—always with reservations in each particular case—the kind of family relationships that surround him or have surrounded him: whether, for example, affection is or is not present in those relationships, if there is interpersonal communication, etc. Emotions have an undeniable relational dimension: they open us up to others, but they may close us to them on occasion. It is true that in given stages or ages of life, during adolescence, for example, emotional conflicts generate problems in family relationships that one has to be able to live through and overcome.

The family is defined as a life project, "a project of love that persists in time and marks the biography of the persons involved."[9] It is not surprising, then, that family relationships have taken a central place in recent years in research on the family from different perspectives.[10]

a) On one side we find a body of psychological and sociological research focusing on the development of the child.[11] Analyzing these works, we can observe the growing interest in the subject of social policy. But few studies focus positively on what parents should do to

9. Cf. F. Altarejos, M. Martínez, M. R. Buxarrais, and A. Bernal, *Familia, valores y educación*, XXIII Seminario Interuniversitario de Teoría de la Educación, Santiago, (2004), 28.

10. I want to thank Professor Robert Constable of Loyola University in Chicago for his valuable suggestions on this point, which helped me to situate the problem, as expressed in the text that follows.

11. The *Heritage Foundation*, for example, gathered studies concerning the family. Cf. its web site: *heritage.org/research/features/familydatabase/results/cfm*.

educate effectively. The answer to that question can be inferred negatively by observing problems.

b) "Effective education" has been discussed in many papers about family relationships. A review of some 2,500 studies points to the direct participation of the parents in the education of their children as one of the essential components of effective education; other elements are ineffective without it.[12] In addition, these studies demonstrate the influence of parents in the development of the character, sociability, academic proficiency, etc., of the children.[13] The findings support what common sense and experience have shown.

c) On the other side, we find a body of doctrine and research, derived from the work of J. Bowlby,[14] known as the "theory of attachment." It is based on the existence of secure maternal relationships in the family, as the key to later relationships with others that are flexible, cordial, firm, without problems, well based. This line of thought has had considerable subsequent development, also with empirical studies.[15]

---

12. Cf. H. J. Walberg, "Improving the Productivity of America's Schools," *Educational Leadership*, 41 (8), (1984): 19-27; M. C. Wang, G. D. Haertl, and H. J. Walberg, *Building Educational Resilience* (Bloomington, IN: Phi Delta Kappa Educational Foundation, 1998); H. J. Walberg, J. Lai, "Meta-analytic Effects of Policy," in G. J. Cizek, ed., *Handbook of Educational Policy* (San Diego, CA: Academic, 1999): 418-454; S. L. Christenson, S. M. Sheridan, *Schools and Families: Creating Essential Connections for Learning* (New York: The Guilford Press, 2001).

13. K. M. Harris, F. Furstenberg, and J. Marmer, "Parental Involvement with Adolescents in Intact Families: The Influence of Fathers over the Life Course," *Demography*, 35 (1998): 201-216.

14. Cf. J. Bowlby, *La separación* (Buenos Aires: Paidós, 1997); Idem, *El vínculo afectivo* (Barcelona: Paidós, 1997).

15. Cf. for example: P. Erdman, T. Caffery, *Attachment and Family Systems* (New York: Brunner-Routledge, 2001).

d) Finally, gathering the results of empirical research and experience, educators and family therapists point out several points for adequate action by parents with reference to the children's education. For instance:[16]

1. Consistency in parents' expectations concerning their children, both together and individually.
2. Close relationship between the parents and with each child. Neither father nor mother should have a closer relationship with the child than with his/her spouse.
3. Sense of responsibility of parents about new situations that arise. Addressing them according to the developmental level of the child, respecting his or her personality and concrete circumstances.
4. The action of the parents should be fundamentally positive.
5. It is good to exercise some supervision over external influences: friends, school, and media.

I would like to focus on a point present in one way or another in studies that focus on familial relationships ("attachment," the necessary tasks of parents, self-esteem, etc.), considering it from a different perspective than that of the studies. The issue is "trust," closely related to respect as a fundamental characteristic of family relationships, a way of "feeling at home" that greatly favors the family's becoming what it is called to be—"the seedbed of society"—by helping develop the sociability of person (including adaptation and openness, socialization and solidarity).

---

16. Cf. R. Turner, *Family Interaction* (New York: John Wiley & Sons, 1970); R. Constable, D. B. Lee, *Social Work with Families: Content and Process* (Chicago: Lyceum Books, 2004).

3. TRUST

3.1. The broad meaning of confidence

The word *home* helps us situate the question we are going to deal with next. The home is the framework determined by family relationships within which they develop.[17]

"Home" [hearth in Spanish] means, in one sense, a place where fire is found—in the kitchen, fireplace, furnace, etc.—but it also signifies house or residence, or family, a group of related persons living together. In this way, house and family seem to be closely associated with the idea of warmth—the warmth that heats a room and cooks food. Similarly, there is a close tie between "hearth" or "home" and the sociological term "environment."[18]

An indispensable condition for a home environment is trust. This rich concept has several meanings, some are elevated and ennobling, so that one can speak of "firm hope in a person or thing," or of the "strength for acting." But there are other meanings, as in "to trust somebody with one's wealth, a secret, or anything else," and "trusting in oneself," whose connotation is not entirely positive and easily degenerates into presumption or "vanity."

These last meanings, paradoxically, seem to lead to suspicion and lack of trust. Isn't it dangerous to entrust something valuable to the good faith of another? What about "trusting him as far as I can throw him"? But is it possible to have a home, an environment of daily living together, without trust? Sad as it is, mistrust is a common experience in society, but it is absolutely at odds with the genuine interpersonal relationships proper to the family.

---

17. Cf. from a different perspective, the recent article of S. Mallet, "Understanding Home: A Critical Review of the Literature," *The Sociological Review*, 52 (1), (2004): 62-89.

18. Cf. Chapter I, Section 4.

To trust is to hope with firmness and security. We speak, for example, of confiding *in* someone, having confidence *in* someone, which implies opening up with that person. This is the basis of friendship. We may speak, also, of confidence in the future, as a hopeful attitude. We value the person we can trust for his qualities, his honesty, for being a trustworthy person; and this leads us to ask ourselves what inspires this confidence or trust. At least we can say that we trust someone who is professionally competent, honest, and shows sincere interest in the well being of others. Trust is not achieved through communication strategies, although these can help; it comes with doing things well, being consistent and sincere. Nor should we make the mistake of confusing what is and what seems—even though these days perception has largely replaced reality, so that it counts for more to seem good than to do good.

What can provide security to the child, to the person? Love—the discovery of the gift received, the gratuitous giving from which he has benefited. In the origin of a family, love is always present: even more, the family is a project of love that is the root of the confidence that prevails in it. The relationships present in it—paternity, maternity, filiation, brotherhood, etc.—demonstrate that reality if they are authentic, as is also seen in the generation of new lives.

At the root of trust we find love, giving; and love and giving are not possible without trust. This is the natural environment of the family, a place where we know ourselves loved for who we are, just for being, and not for our way of being this way or that. And this is so for the young and the old, the healthy and the sick. There is a natural relationship among members of the family that is not the result of choice; and from the beginning of his or her life, a child learns to be a person in his or her relationship with other people.[19]

---

19. Cf. R. Buttiglione, *La persona y la familia* (Madrid: Palabra, 1999).

Here the child learns that he does not exist in isolation but is related to others necessarily. His goodness is intimately united to the goodness of others; he has obligations which are natural consequences of having been born of certain parents, not the result of a contract or a consensus. To see family relationships from that perspective would be to miss their nature and would make it difficult to "feel at home."

A father, for instance, does not care for his small daughter or son or his elderly mother because of a contract or because of their good qualities; but simply because they are who they are: his daughter, his son, his mother.

In this way, family relationships can be an extraordinary school of generosity and altruism. If I love my parents or my siblings, and seek the best for them, it is not for their personal characteristics but simply for being who they are. This usually causes family members to feel a great sense of security—and also responsibility, knowing that one is the object of the love and trust of the others.

"Trust is an action that springs from the right use of freedom, which cannot stop applying to others what we would like to have applied to us. Thus, it is also the fruit of responsibility, because confidence, then, is nothing else than the positive projection of a first practical principle which recognizes the natural idea: 'Don't do to the other what we would not like to be done to us.' "[20]

3.2. Confidence and truthfulness

Confidence is rooted also in truthfulness, which gives substance to the person who communicates truthfully as well as to the one who receives that truthful communication. In the family

---

20. F. Altarejos, C. Naval, J. L. González-Simancas, "*La confianza: exigencia de la libertad personal*," in A. Malo, ed., *La dignitá della persona humana* (Rome: Edizioni Università della Santa Croce, 2003): 238.

environment people show themselves as they are, with no need for disguises and masks; and if there are any they vanish naturally in the face of intimacy and close relationships, which dictates that a person comes to be known as he is not so much by what he says as by what he does.[21]

Truthfulness is openness, sharing, vital authenticity without concealment of reality. In some cases, it overcomes resistance to showing things as they are. It is, in the end, daring to be what one is, without fear. The attitude of respect for truth, basic to happiness and to living together, finds in the family a privileged opportunity for apprenticeship.

In addition, as Newman argued so accurately[22] in his *Grammar of Assent*, to know the truth and know that it is true generates certainty, security, and confidence: "This is an essential characteristic of certainty over any issue: to be fully certain that such idea will remain, but to be certain, also, that even if it should fail, the thing itself about which we are certain, be it whatever it is, will remain exactly as it is, true and irreversible." This reasoning could be applied to different aspects of the family, to family relationships, to the knowledge and interaction between members of a family that so often become the focus of small problems, typical of life together. There is confidence in the persons—beyond any utilitarian outlook—although they seem not to respond, even if they fail and make mistakes: there is always a deeper truth, always hope that the person can change. At the root of trust we find the conviction that a human being can improve.

---

21. Cf. Romano Guardini, *Virtú* (Brescia, Italy: Morcelliana, 1997).

22. "Certitude is"—says Newman—"the perception of a truth united to the perception that it is a truth, or to the conscience of knowing, as expressed in the phrase 'I know that I know' or 'I know that I know that I know'—or simply 'I know,' because a simple reflexive statement of the mind over the I summarizes all the series of self-conscience, without need of an effective development of them" J. H. Newman, *Persuadido por la Verdad* (Madrid: Encuentro, 1995): 57.

3.3 *Shyness and resentment*

But bad experiences unavoidably raise a question: what should one do when confidence is lost, when expectations are disappointed and one has the sense of being betrayed? Loss of confidence, disappointment, lack of trust—these are hard to deal with and even harder to live with it. Then there is no real answer but forgiveness.

At that point diffidence and resentment will creep in (within the family or outside of it, but if inside, harder to deal with). These are not the same, because the diffident person closes himself off while the resentful one feels hurt.

Diffidence is an internal stiffening that paralyzes and hardens, although at times it disguises itself in a remarkable external activity that is a kind of fleeing from the situation and is difficult to overcome.[23]

Max Scheler says resentment is a psychic self-intoxication.[24] It is the reaction to something felt as an offense or an aggression that hurts us. It may be caused by an action, an omission, or by a given circumstance that makes one resentful (perhaps a defect or a disease). The reaction may have a real or imaginary cause; and if it is real, it may be exaggerated by the one who suffers it. The difficulty lies in the fact that the resentment or distrust is found at the emotional level, with the difficulties that accompany it, because we "feel hurt." At times the cause of the resentment may not be clear; and at other times the reasons may justify such a response, which reinforces the resentment.

This situation can be overcome in friendships or in the family. Sometimes it is enough to realize that the reaction was

23. Cf. F. Ugarte, *Del resentimiento al perdón. Una puerta a la felicidad* (Madrid: Rialp, 2004).

24. M. Scheler, *El resentimiento en la moral* (Madrid: Caparrós Editores, 1993): 23.

excessive or that the offense nonexistance.[25] But the resentful person has trouble reasoning like this, precisely because he "re-senses" the offense, does not forget, and deepens the wound, adding sorrow to it, while keeping vivid and alive something that may have happened years before. A character that is insecure, reserved, sensitive, and sentimental can contribute to this, but it reveals a weak will, an emotional life focused on the self, and at times an imagination out of touch with reality.[26]

The direct way to escape resentment and distrust is to excuse (when there is no guilt or intention to hurt on the part of the supposed offender) or to forgive. But it is important to realize that forgiving is at the level of the will. It is an act of love, not feelings. I can decide to forgive in spite of my feeling of being injured or my lingering memory of the offense, still there despite my efforts to forget. Only one capable of love is capable of forgiving, of being able to seek even the good of the offender.[27] One of the best antidotes against mistrust and resentment is precisely gratitude, which proceeds from awareness of the good things we possess.

3.4. Acceptance, dialogue, and respect

We have spoken of the root of trust and the danger of mistrust. Now let us consider how trust is manifested in family relationships. Of the many aspects we could mention, I shall refer only to three: acceptance, dialogue, and respect.

---

25. G. Marañón states that "Man reacts with direct energy to aggression and expels, automatically, as a foreign body, the ruing from his conscience. This saving elasticity does not exist in the one who is resented." [*Tiberio. Historia de un resentido* (Madrid: Espasa-Calpe, 1981): 29].

26. Polo says, and it could also be applied here, that "the person is not a center, but rather a capacity of centering oneself, of giving oneself without losing oneself." [L. Polo, *La persona humana y su crecimiento* (Pamplona, Spain: EUNSA, 1996): 26].

27. Cf. C. S. Lewis, *The Weight of Glory* (New York: Harper Collins, 2001).

First of all, acceptance of oneself and others, of the diversity hidden in each of us. Acceptance presupposes recognition (to love is to affirm the other for being who he or she is) and is the basis of sharing (to accept giving). This is the source of the sociable dimension of the person.[28]

Trust is also manifested in dialogue, the inter-subjective communication provided by family relationships. Nobody ignores the difficulties found in practice, especially in particular circumstances (for example, the stressful situation of parents due to their workload[29] or because of the changes of adolescence experienced by a teenager[30]) but that is no reason for refusing to seek dialogue.

Seneca, in his perceptive *Epístolas a Lucilio,* says that such trust is characteristic of friendship: the true quality of friend is present in one to whom, after finding him worthy, we confide secrets as if he were our alter ego.[31] What reasons can we have to hide news in the presence of a friend?

"Some tell," says Seneca (and in the family this is easily understood) "to anyone who comes along what should be told only to friends and complain of what bothers them to anybody at all. Others, on the contrary, are reluctant to make confidences, even to those they love best, and like people who do not even trust themselves, hide every secret within them.

---

28. Polaino says that mature persons are characterized by: a) feeling comfortable with themselves; b) having good perceptions of others; and c) being capable of confronting the demands of life; Cf. A. Polaino, *Familia y autoestima* (Barcelona: Ariel, 2003): 56.

29. Stress in the family can cause general violence, or at least, irritability, short tempers, etc. (Cf. ibid., 250); a situation that we have to recognize on time, before it can lead to family conflicts.

30. Adolescence is a key moment in which affective education and capacity to open oneself up are forged. Habitually the adolescent—states Polanco (ibid., 172 and ff), loves himself, wants to love others, and wants to be loved (although at times, he or she does not feel loved).

31. Cf. Séneca, *Epístolas morales a Lucilio. I, (Libros I-IX; Epístolas 1-80)* (Madrid: Gredos, 1986), *Epístola* I, 3.

Neither the one thing nor the other should be done, because both are defective."[32] So that this dialogue may take place, a prior step is necessary: the presence of real togetherness.

Finally, trust is manifested in respect. This is a genuine social disposition that allows each one to be what he can achieve. At times we have a negative view of respect, as mere abstention, but it is more than that: it is granting autonomy; it means accepting in the other and recognizing value in that which we do not understand.

3.5. Confidence, hope, and freedom

We have seen the root of trust and how it is shown in family relationships. Now we must ask what generates confidence among members of the family and what it contributes to shaping sociability in societies of which the person is part. We have already seen several references to this question; now we shall add some others.

Trust generates *hope*. To trust is to hope firmly and surely, as was said before, while at the same time the knowledge that somebody trusts us spurs us to greater efforts in order not to disappoint those who extend this trust. Absence of this relationship in the family is a serious setback for a child, experienced in different ways: lack of enthusiasm, suspicion, apathy, hopelessness, etc. From another perspective, however, one sees that overprotection generates affective dependency, which also causes personality problems.[33]

Trust produces and sustains an active attitude of welcoming, and promotes a hospitable mood in interpersonal relations. It is more than just being present; it involves openness and

---

32. Ibid., I, 3, 4, p. 101.

33. Polaino refers to this pathological case as a general and excessive need of care, leading to submission, adhesion, and fear of separation, beginning at the start of adulthood. It is found in several contexts (*Familia y autoestima*, 63).

availability of one person to the other, in time of need and time of joy, which also must be shared for maximum enjoyment. The "hospitable" personality is sought equally on sad or joyful occasions, both of which are necessary for the harmonious maturing of the self. A deep welcoming attitude is manifested in three "small" qualities or dispositions, viewed as desirable in social dealings: cordiality, amiability, and affability. The three together are the essence of courtesy.

Today a peculiar social sensitivity clumsily dismisses courtesy in favor of the supposedly greater value of spontaneity or naturalness. Courtesy is considered to be artificial. But authentic courtesy is not dry and formal; it is akin to cordiality, amiability, and affability. Courtesy, says the dictionary, is "the act that manifests attention, respect or affection of one person to another." Only a selfish, cold person considers it an obligation imposed from without rather than a "cordial" effusion (from Latin *cor/cordis*: heart), flowing from the heart. Someone who communicates affection with promptness and delicacy deserves to be loved: he is "amiable" or "affable"—someone you can talk with, a rare trait in these times.

Trust, correctly understood, promotes and is required by freedom. Only in a climate of trust can one act freely, without fear of being wrong or failing; only thus can one take risks, accept danger, and, precisely because the others are free and capable of improving and of changing, confide in them. Responsibility is called a consequence of freedom, understood in reference to personal growth. At present there is a widespread and imprecise notion of freedom that sees it as boundless independence. This is the confused idea that the fullness of freedom is "liberation": I am truly free when I can throw aside whatever makes me dependent on something or someone. From this libertarian viewpoint, obviously, no binding commitment is acceptable, because it acts as an impediment that limits the future via the dependence thus generated. In this view, to accept responsibility for what one does is an obvious contradiction of freedom. And yet, dominion over ourselves, generated by truly free actions, is not possible unless we accept them and their consequences. If we understand freedom properly, it is not spontaneity without any limits or total indeterminacy, but a capacity for binding self-determination,[34] with responsibility as its inseparable complement.

However, freedom has another dimension: not that of personal growth, which is responsibility, but that of obligation toward the persons with whom I have personal relationships. And that, precisely, is trust.

One can speak a great deal, with eloquence, about the dignity of the human being; but it is insulting if our actions manifest a generalized distrust of others. As confidence generates confidence, so distrust of others provokes distrust toward us. This is the death of interpersonal relationships. Without trust one cannot help improve the other—cannot, that is, contribute effectively to his or her education.

3.6. Hope, basis for the exercise of authority and sociability

Trust also is the basis for the "exercise of authority." This demand is based on caring, on the search for the good, for the good of the whole family. One helps and corrects others because one loves them, and in this way affection not only is shown but increased, while the one who helps also learns. In this project of love that is the family, the members' actions and omissions have decisive influence in shaping the lives of each and, specifically, their social dispositions.

If the child sees other members of the family as a part of himself—his closest neighbors—and learns to care for them, he

---

34. The meanings of "freedom from" and "freedom for" are discussed in the next chapter (Cf. Chapter 6, Section 1).

is in effect learning how to care for others not so close, thus enlarging the circle through caring for his family. The transition is more natural from "care for those who are mine" to "care for others, farther way," than from "care for myself" to "care for others, farther away." Caring for one's family in the circumstances of ordinary life is the best training in caring for others.

Relations of affection and authority within the family can be a natural school where parents and children learn to govern and be governed, to command and obey. The problem is how to pass from the home to society, the broader community. Trust in the environment of the family is indispensable element to this.

Two manifestations of that confidence in family relationships deserve to be noted.

a) It eases adaptation to a group.

b) It expands into the social virtues tied to solidarity or, as some prefer to call it, altruism, as a personal project.[35] One learns to give gratuitously what one has received gratuitously, configuring social dispositions in the form of piety, honor, truthfulness, liberality, gratitude, the desire to make restitution where there is unfairness, friendship, cordiality, acceptance of legitimate authority, obedience to fair rules.

In this way family life can contribute to humanizing society. The result is societies that are more human, more personal, more participatory and, in the end, a well-grounded sociability based on deep respect for the person.

---

35. F. Altarejos, A. Rodríguez, and J. Fontrodona, *Retos educativos de la globalización* (Pamplona: EUNSA, 2003): 174-196; L. Polo, *Quién es el hombre*, 5th ed. (Madrid: Rialp, 2003); C. Naval, *Educar ciudadanos*, 1995.

CHAPTER 6

EDUCATION IN FREEDOM AND AFFECTIVITY

(Gerardo Castillo Ceballos)

1. EDUCATIONAL PRACTICE OF FREEDOM IN THE FAMILY

There are two kinds of human behavior: reactive, related to the satisfaction of needs, and effusive or expansive, related to being a person—behavior not determined by a prior need but an expression of freedom, the fundamental quality of the person. Freedom is an interior energy that allows one to open up to the world of people and serve them out of love, and to the world of things, which one dominates through knowledge.[1]

My freedom is primarily a "freedom for" (to do good); but that freedom is linked to a "freedom from," which lies in overcoming conditionings or interior limitations that prevent me from reaching good ends. Freedom is actualized by a decision to pursue the good, inasmuch as choosing evil is neither freedom nor partial freedom, although it may be a sign of freedom.[2]

---

1. J. Choza, *La supresión del pudor* (Pamplona: EUNSA, 1980): 107.
2. St. Thomas Aquinas: *De Veritate*, q. 22, a. 6.

Freedom is a gift we have received that can and must grow. It is a personal conquest tied to its good use, which is shown by making good decisions and the attainment of what we have decided. For that reason, it is important to teach persons how to decide, and to create the habit of making decisions.[3]

This is one of the main reference points of the educational action of parents and teachers: how to help their children or pupils grow in freedom and develop a pattern of positive free choices over time.

1.1. Freedom behavior

To educate for freedom implies encouraging freedom of behavior. For that, the authentic educator (parent or teacher) is not one who makes himself indispensable to the pupil, but one who knows how to make him or herself less and less necessary (according to the age of the child or student).

Man is born free, but without knowing how to use his freedom. He is a victim of internal limitations to freedom: for example, ignorance, sloth, selfishness, love of comfort, rigidity. He is reluctant to make personal decisions and to accept the consequences of his actions. He tends to do what he likes and desires and not what he truly wants, or should want. For that reason his freedom needs to be educated, from the earliest years, in the family environment.

To educate is to liberate. This obviously is not the false liberation of those who simply do as their instincts or whims dictate. Such people believe they are liberated, free, because they do just as they like, whatever their body asks of them at any moment. For this kind of person, moral norms are prejudices to be overcome; they believe that by freeing themselves of norms, they become free persons. But the opposite happens: they become slaves of their wrongful inclinations.

3. F. Otero, *La libertad en la familia* (Pamplona: EUNSA, 1982): 26-27.

Essentially, to be free is not to free oneself from something, in the sense of breaking all bonds and shirking duties. To be free is to be free *for* something. "Initial freedom, what we will call *liberation*, is devoid of meaning if it is not in reference to terminal freedom, what we will call the *end-plan* or *project*. Freedom, in this way, is not only the quality of not being physically obligated to do anything (liberation), but the capacity to obligate oneself to something (a plan of one's own will) . . . . Detached from such a plan, freedom is an empty and useless concept. . . . The plan or project, on the contrary, is anticipatory, as is genuine freedom."[4]

In authentic liberation, all the ties that keep us from having control of ourselves are broken. Those educated in freedom learn over time to direct their own lives.

So-called "personalized education points to this great educational objective. The expression has been widely popularized by García Hoz: "Personalized education responds to the attempt to stimulate the subject so that he will perfect his 'capacity to direct his own life,' in other words, develop his capacity to make his personal freedom effective, participating in the life of the community with his own special characteristics."[5]

Life for many people consists in allowing themselves to be carried along by circumstances and events. It is matter of adapting, accepting in a passive and comfortable way, the ready-made life others give them. It is a state of permanent indecision, life with no goals. Such people do not want to be the main protagonists of their own lives.

In today's society, adolescents and young adults have numerous "invitations" to leave the direction of their lives in someone else's hands (for example, an ideologue or a false friend). They may take to the invitation if they have not learned to direct their own lives.

---

4. C. Llano, *Las formas actuales de la libertad* (México City: Trillas, 1983): 25-27.

5. V. García-Hoz, *Educación personalizada* (Madrid: Rialp, 1988): 18.

To learn to conduct one's own life consists in attaining the capacity to govern oneself. In the concrete, it means knowing how to choose the best course of action in each situation, and at each moment, from among the possible alternatives. Educators need to ask themselves which model of education best points toward the goal of self-government. In my opinion, the most adequate model is that which González-Simancas refers to as growth in various dimensions—progressive self-orientation toward the fullest possible development, the development of personal freedom.

This growth refers to self-dominion: self-knowledge and the making of decisions.

It is above all, growth in one's inner life. All this implies "growing in our capacity for initiative and creativity, which leads to personal plans filled with aspirations, demanding exertion of thought and acts of the will, involving our heart, our affections, our most noble sentiments."[6]

To direct is to point one's intentions and actions towards a determined end, so as to get intended results. This implies making plans aimed at what we want to attain.

To direct one's own life means, to a large degree, planning it in its different aspects: family, work, culture, social relationships, free time, etc. Man is unique in being able to choose the future he wants and undertake to convert the choice into reality. Human life is anticipation, realization of the future: getting something done that otherwise would not.

But not just any plan of one's life is useful. Among the conditions that must be met, I note these three:

1) That it be based on a correct interpretation of life (a form of life that does not contradict the dignity of the person).

---

6. J. L. González-Simancas, *Educación, libertad y compromiso* (Pamplona: EUNSA, 1992): 31-32.

2) That it not be self-contradictory, that it have internal consistency.

3) That it consider others, manifest solidarity, not be self-centered.

Youth (about 17 to 25 years) is the time for developing one's first life project. This will be a comprehensive project dealing with state in life and future occupation as well as the general orientation of one's life, from the point of view of values.

At the time of elaborating this project, the young person must consider its quality. The project must express the most intimate and noble aspirations of the person. It will be, then, a project for a good life.

A good life plan will show that one knows what one aspires to in life (without confusing it simply with what one likes and wants).

Some life plans implicitly include a commitment for life (for example, a plan to marry).

A mature and responsible person will be loyal to his project or plan. This entails a commitment.

To learn to direct one's life includes the capacity to carry out what has been projected. Each person needs fortitude and perseverance (acts of the will) to bring to fruition what has been proposed, given that the realization of any project implies overcoming difficulties.

The young need personal orientation to formulate good projects and bring them to term. The hope is that they will be able to solve the problems of their life, which includes:

- choice of profession
- preparation for that profession
- use of free time
- developing friendships
- facing family responsibilities

• entering into social relationships.

The different aspects of life just mentioned apply to every person, but each one must shape his or her own life in relation to them. Because of that, it is not enough in education to deal with general situations. Parents must help each child know himself or herself better (capacities, limitations, interests, character, etc.), know the situation in which he has to act (study, work, family, etc.), and make well-thought-out, realistic personal decisions.

It is a good idea to propose to the young that they make plans for the near and the distant future: plans for study, work, use of free time, Christian formation, etc. It is also advisable to give them numerous opportunities to solve by themselves the problems that emerge in carrying out each plan or project.

In the current environment of the "easy life," parents often make the mistake of satisfying almost all their children's desires. For that reason, González-Simancas proposes that they should encourage them to look forward to things instead of giving them everything ready-made. He explains:

"The best way to educate for enthusiasm, joyfulness, and optimism, characteristics needed to live happily, is 'to turn desires into a plan', create situations in which learners—and also we, the educators—look ahead joyfully to the plan's realization, no matter how elementary or ordinary: perhaps a small thing, a simple plan, that will take on the significance of something enthusiastically awaited, among other reasons because it involves us personally, implying a challenge to our intellect and our creativity, to our capacity to overcome obstacles."[7]

Consider an example. A son wants to improve his knowledge of a second language by spending some summers in a foreign country. His parents suggest he make a plan in which he considers the following.

---

7. Ibid., 105.

- The best place (country, city): This must be a place where he will be able to practice the language chosen and so properly use his time in reference to the objective sought.

- Proper living arrangements (residence, family, etc.): more important than material conditions is that there be a good moral environment and that he be with good companions.

- Financing the trip and life away from home: saving money; looking into job possibilities where he is going to live, etc.

The parents can and must give advice. But in my opinion they should not choose the place or lodgings without considering the preferences of the child. Nor should they solve the financial problems (they can help, but not so much that the child does not have to look for some money needed).

Parents who solve all the difficulties of their children prevent them from having a valuable experience in learning how to arrange their own lives. Education is not directing children's lives. It is creating situations with problems to be solved and letting the children solve them.

Life itself is a problem that demands struggle and personal effort. Children who are not trained in solving problems are at risk of becoming inadequate people as adults—people who will be overwhelmed by the first difficulty.

1.2. Personal fulfillment of children

One of the main causes of the lack of integration into their families of many adolescent children is the understanding of personal fulfillment as "self-realization," equivalent to self-sufficiency.

Hervada has pointed that the prefix "self" indicates that the realization is not directed toward an end. It is not seen as involving pre-established goals set by a superior being; rather, "man determines his own plan of life for himself, that is, he 'self-realizes'; he realizes himself." At bottom, this is life lived without a goal and without norms.

The same author adds that self-realization means total autonomy in planning one's existence as well as in achieving what is projected. This unlimited autonomy has limiting effects: "Once the idea of goal is lost, man becomes enclosed in himself, because a being without finality will not project himself in a straight line but only as a circle that revolves about him." Hervada proposes the example of a car incapable of going toward a destination. Even with the motor running, it cannot go anywhere, it only runs in place.[8]

Man enclosed in himself is unable to forget himself. This, in time, prevents his projecting himself toward others to serve them. It is a crucial limitation, given that man realizes himself, perfects himself, not by remaining alone within himself, but insofar as he unites himself to a good that transcends him and surpasses him.

Victor Frankl states that the principal motivation of man is the struggle to find a meaning in life. He calls this the "will to meaning." It is not a matter of inventing the meaning of life but discovering it outside oneself: "The true meaning of life must be found in the world, and not inside the human being or inside his own mind, as if he were dealing with a closed system."

On this premise, Frankl concludes that self-realization cannot itself be a goal of life: "The more man makes an effort to reach it, the more it flees from him, because only insofar as man makes a commitment to fulfill the meaning of his life does he self-realize himself. In other words, the self-realization cannot be reached when it is considered an end in

---

8. J. Hervada, *Diálogos sobre el amor y el matrimonio* (Pamplona: EUNSA, 1987): 73–75.

itself, but only when it is taken as a secondary effect of one's own transcendence."[9]

"Self-realization" as an end in itself is no more than narcissistic self-contemplation. It is an exaltation of one's own "I" that leads to shedding commitments and responsibilities and this hindering true personal development. A human being must be open to others. This is a necessary condition for culture and personal growth. Its contrary lead to closing oneself in, treating oneself as a thing (reifying oneself), and living a fanatical individualism.

A person realizes himself by fulfilling the plan (project) of his existence, fulfilling the goals for which he has been created: the natural end or project of existence imprinted in human nature (which is concretized in partial ends related to work, life in one's family, etc.); and the supernatural end or project (plan) of existence involved in the salvific plan of God.

True realization lies in reaching personal perfection. It is a deliberate perfecting of the person in accord with his ends.

Why does it take such a long time for human beings to accomplish this? Are human persons imperfect realities? Does the person constitute himself a person by acting?

The person is a complete or perfect being in itself. Each man or woman, by being a person, has an original dignity or perfection. This original greatness is a gift from God that involves no merit on the part of the individual.

The deepest foundation of human dignity resides in the fact that man is an image of God and is ordained to God. Man is a being for God, from whom he receives his perfection.

Man discovers the sense of his dignity insofar as he discovers that he is free. Being free allows him to choose between diverse alternatives: he can act or not act; he can act in one way or another. Here resides the superiority of man over the animals:

---

9. V. Frankl, *El hombre en busca de sentido* (Barcelona: Herder, 1983): 109.

the actions of animals flow necessarily from the nature they have received. (A hungry man can eat less than he wants and can even postpone the time of eating; an animal, on the contrary, can do only what instinct tells it to do: in this case, to eat).

If a man's use of freedom can affect him, the man, in some way, is "making himself" as he lives. Professor Millán Puelles says: "We are free, that is, we are not fully made; but we are, which means that not everything has yet to be done." But if I am not fully made, I must make myself: "Willingly or unwillingly, man is a task for himself: the task of making himself a man."[10]

A human being is born with freedom, together with a personal end, which he must approach progressively, step by step. Freely doing that is realizing oneself. As long as one has further to go, one is not yet a fully realized person; there is more to be learned, improvement yet to be made.

Freedom applied to making oneself confers on the individual a second dignity that is truly meritorious. It consists in making one's daily behavior appropriate to one's end or the plan of existence impressed into one's nature—or, in living consistently with what one is according to one's original dignity.

Pindar's imperative expresses it very well: "Become what you are." That is to say: freely become, by your activity and your effort, what you are in a natural way. This is equivalent to wanting God's will and constitutes the object of education: to conform human freedom to the demands of human nature.

The task of "making oneself man" is a process of self-possession. There is no authentic realization of self without dominion over self, which is self-possession and liberation from selfish tendencies. Dominion over self makes one freer, with a greater capacity to love.

---

10. A. Millán Puelles, *Sobre el hombre y la sociedad* (Madrid: Rialp, 1976): 230.

1.3. The family as primary environment for personal fulfillment

Although personal realization is something that happens "within" the person who accomplishes it (he is the protagonist of the process), that person needs to find situations that will allow him to act and to relate—that will allow him to exercise his freedom.

We may talk, then, of areas of personal realization. Among these we recognize five: professional work, family, friendships, social relations, and leisure time. These five areas allow the person to achieve realization in the family (being a good wife or husband, good father or mother, good child), in work (being a competent and responsible professional), in friendships (being a good friend), in social life (being a good citizen), in free time (developing his personality through leisure activities). Each aspect of realization must be seen in relation to integral realization, not as something independent, for the person is an indivisible whole.

It would make no sense, for example, to place a premium on responsible behavior of a professional man who was also an irresponsible father. It would not be correct to consider work as oriented exclusively to results, forgetting human relationships and service to others. By the same token, it would not be proper to understand free time as an opportunity for evading responsibilities. The aim is to see all situations as opportunities for personal improvement.

Granted that all five of these areas are necessary and important, it is appropriate to emphasize the special possibilities of two: work and family.

If professional work is done in freedom (with a personal style and as a protagonist, with self-direction; a service spirit, etc.) it becomes a prime means of personal realization. But on the whole, the family is its main arena. Why is this so?

First of all, it is because of the close relationship between person and family. The family is a "natural institution in which one is born, grows, and dies as a person."[11] Each child needs the personal contact proper to the family: to be loved because he *is* (because he exists), not for *what he is*; to be considered *someone* and not *something* (as stated in chapter 4). This is so:

- from before birth—being expected and received with the love that a person needs;
- during life—to be listened to, understood, propelled, and encouraged to grow as a person;
- at the end of life—to be helped to a good death, to die as a person, in a loving environment.

This need of the person for the family led Pope John Paul II to state that "human existence has a familial character." This points to a vision of man as a relational being and to the family as a framework of interpersonal relationships; in the end, it is an affirmation of coexistence as something radical in anthropology, as noted earlier.

Another way to make this point is to say the family is the atmosphere a person needs to breathe. This special atmosphere is characterized by love: the family is a community of persons united by bonds of unconditional love, growing together. The family community finds its deepest foundation in a typical capacity of man: to love in a familial way.

When the need for the family is questioned, the reply is that it is not mainly for reproduction, although this typical function is widely accepted (see chapter 1). It can, of course, take place outside of the family; but it should take place in the loving environment provided by the family, which is most adequate to the dignity of the human person.

---

11. J. L. Vildarich, *El modelo antropológico del matrimonio* (Madrid: Rialp, 2001): 110.

The family is the main area of personal realization for a second reason: it is an environment in which one discovers and lives true values.

Personal realization consists of growing in one's values. Values necessary for this personal growth because they are specifications of the good. Values encourage man to a continuous surpassing of his limitations.

Man "finds his being" only insofar as he discovers true values, makes a commitment to them, and lives his life in light of such values.

In other environments different from the family, values can be transmitted (for example, at school). But that is limited to giving information about values. What makes the family special is that it is a place where values are acquired by being lived.

Persons are not primarily educated by speeches, lectures, or books. What educates is belonging to a community with a good way of life: an authentic culture, a formative character.

Virtue cannot be taught (Socrates) so much through words, as through actions. Virtues are acquired in educational communities in which authentic values are alive, and available for internalization.

There is a way of learning within the family that does not exist outside it. This is learning by absorbing the adult way of life. From the earliest age, children learn, as if by osmosis, what they see and hear at home: criteria, customs, manners, norms of behavior. Beyond everyday experiences lie values.

Learning by absorption is possible only in a community that lives together with such intensity, in informal relationships, where people behave spontaneously and naturally, where each person feels loved for himself and not for what he does or has. It is fundamental to locate an authentic educational environment in the family.

1.4. *Growing in freedom*

Education for freedom requires giving children or students opportunities to learn to grow in freedom at the different stages of their life.

Strictly speaking, education for freedom starts in adolescence, with the awakening of the personality (the discovery of the "I", the birth of intimacy, the development of personal identity). Unlike the child, the adolescent is very concerned about his freedom, which he at first equates with mere unlimited independence.

In a broad sense, learning the use of freedom can and must start in the third stage of childhood (7 to 10 years of age, approximately). This is a time of emotional stability, curiosity, activity, and adaptation to home and school. In this period, children are often highly receptive to almost everything proposed or taught by parents or teachers, whom they still assign high prestige.

F. Otero underscores that "the third stage of childhood is the great opportunity to educate for freedom, because it is a period of childhood maturity when it is possible to teach children how to think, how to become informed, how to decide and to accomplish what has been decided; when it is possible to develop easy behavior, initiative, self-control, the disposition to serve, autonomy, responsibility, the capacity to choose or accept. At the same time, one can encourage the effort necessary to overcome such personal limitations as selfishness, ignorance, cowardice, indolence, passivity, clumsiness, rigidity, servility, irresolution, indiscriminate rejection, etc."[12]

Adolescence is, basically, the stage at which biological adulthood (puberty) is reached while psychological and social maturity have yet to come. The whole objective of development

---

12. F. Otero, *La libertad en la familia*, 68.

at this stage is to pass from one stage to the next within a reasonable period of time.

Psychological and social adulthood signify maturity, personal realization, responsible autonomy, ability to decide for oneself and direct one's own life.

Adolescence is a process of growing up linked to the maturation of personal freedom. Adolescents must be invited to move ahead little by little along an inclined plane:

- From dependent to autonomous behavior
- From imitation to original behavior
- From being under another's direction to autonomous morality (not to be confused with moral subjectivism)
- From guardianship to self-government
- From play to work
- From a plan of life drawn up by parents to a personal plan of life designed by the adolescent.

Success in the challenge and adventure of growing up requires that the adolescent child know how to distinguish between right and wrong forms of grownup behavior. To be an adult does not mean (as adolescents often believe) throwing over all norms and rules observed at home in the past and at school; it does not consist of ridding oneself of duties or rejecting the authority of parents and teachers. To be a grownup, it is essential to "grow in responsible freedom." Freedom can and ought to grow during life, but there is a stage in which such growth is more feasible: adolescence, the transition to adult life.

What is responsible freedom? It is the capacity to accept new responsibilities; to do what we do not like, when that is recognized as a duty; to accept the consequences of one's decisions; to answer for one's actions before others.

A good way of encouraging responsible freedom in the adolescent is to confront him with its challenges by raising questions that will make him think.

1) Are you capable of being yourself without being dominated and carried along by what friends suggest?
2) Are you capable of accepting yourself as you are at all times?
3) Can you show yourself to others as you are in reality, without artificial disguises?
4) Can you control yourself or are you carried along passively by your whims?
5) Are you able to think before acting?
6) Are you capable of thinking of what is best for the others, before thinking of what seems best for you?
7) Are you able to accept the small contradictions that arise each day?
8) Can you control your reactions and stay calm when someone or something is being bothersome?
9) Are you capable of solving your problems by yourself, without asking for unnecessary help?

These and other questions can shed light on the idea of freedom, and help in the avoidance of errors and over-simplifications. The adolescent should aspire to the following:

• Committed and unselfish freedom, not only "liberation;"
• Freedom that grows with struggle against interior obstacles (ignorance, lack of information, laziness, lack of initiative, impatience, rigidity, selfishness, etc.);
• Freedom that is not individualism or isolation (learning how to make autonomous conduct compatible with cooperation and the fulfillment of duties);

- Freedom that is not identified with the satisfaction of one's appetites and desires, but with the capacity for self-determination, oriented to doing good.

Together with the questions above, certain things of an educational nature must take place: require adolescents to face the consequences of their actions; accustom them to think and get information before deciding; encourage them to enter into situations which they will have to solve by themselves, without help from parents or teachers.[13]

1.5. The exercise of freedom

1.5.1. Developing self-control

This requires the example of parents and teachers and takes the form of respect, calmness, patience, good humor. In addition, children and students should be taught to overcome limitations opposed to self-control: ignorance, cowardice, lack of effort.

Overcoming ignorance requires teaching the adolescent to be well-informed; to know how to distinguish between quality information and information of questionable value; to learn how to learn; to know how to find good sources of information.

Overcoming cowardice involves encouraging valor. In this way someone can face his own weaknesses and not allow himself to be dominated by others.

1.5.2. Developing the capacity to serve

In addition to giving good example, one must teach children to recognize the reality of service (often children do not recognize what their parents do as service). One must teach them to be thankful and to express thanks by service of their own.

---

13. G. Castillo, *El adolescente y sus retos* (Madrid: Pirámide, 2002).

It will help to provide opportunities to the child or student to render concrete services—and to thank him or her afterwards. Assigning them specific chores is useful.

1.5.3. DEVELOPING THE CAPACITY FOR AUTONOMY
Concerning *external autonomy*, it is useful to grant areas of freedom so that children learn how to organize themselves: for example, in their use of time, in their recreation, in their work. Areas of autonomy need to be expanded according to a child's age and degree of responsibility.

As far as internal autonomy is concerned, it is good to accustom children to accept or reject things in light of correct criteria; to act by themselves (thinking, informing themselves, before deciding and acting).

1.5.4. DEVELOPING THE CAPACITY FOR RESPONSIBILITY
This involves providing children with the opportunity to take responsibility for what they do to others, teaching them to fulfill their chores, making them see the reasons, encouraging them, and sharing enthusiasm with them.

1.5.5. DEVELOPING THE CAPACITY TO DECIDE
Helping children identify the different alternatives among which they may choose. They need to grasp that choosing well may not mean accepting the first option or alternative at hand. One must know what one wants (and choose for the sake of an objective). Children should be taught this through questions: what do you want, what information do you have, etc?

- Be careful not to replace them in this task (don't choose for them).
- Help them evaluate the rightness or the wrongness of each decision that is made.
- Urge them to carry out what they have decided.

2. PRACTICAL EDUCATION OF AFFECTIVITY

2.1. The complexity of affective life

Affective life is considered the least settled part of psychology. *Feelings* are different from knowledge and tendencies. They are psychological phenomena of a subjective sort. They accompany knowledge and tendencies, providing them with a pleasant or unpleasant tone.

J. A. Marina defines feelings as "blocks of integrated information that include valuations in which the subject is implicated and strike the balance between a situation and a predisposition to act."

The same author distinguishes three types of feelings:

1) *Sentimental states:* "lasting sentiments (feelings) that remain stable, while other, more ephemeral feelings change simultaneously. It is convenient to distinguish between sentimental habits (love and hate, for example), which have a permanence that shapes personality, and moods, which have some lasting effect but less consistency."

2) *Emotion:* "a brief feeling, usually appearing suddenly with physical manifestations (agitation, palpitations, pallor, blushing, etc.)."

3) *Passion:* "intense feelings, vehement, tendentious, with a powerful influence over behavior."[14]

Affectivity is of great importance even beyond itself.

• The balance of feeling, between pleasant and unpleasant, determines how happy or unhappy one is.

---

14. J. A. Marina, *El laberinto sentimental* (Barcelona: Anagrama, 1996): 35.

- Feelings are modifiers of knowing (they can speed up the formation of images and favor the memory, for example).

- Feelings stimulate tendencies, mainly of the will, that contribute to the development of motives to act.

- Educated and well-directed feelings are valuable resources for ruling oneself, while disorders of affectivity can produce mental illness and painful complexes.

To understand the affective life of a person is a compelling but difficult challenge. Marina explains why.

- "Feelings render only a partial account of complex situations;

- "Feelings are the conscious reaction to a situation. They are a subjective and objective mix, an urgent summary, experience and language in a code that one has to learn to decode. It is hard to grasp that feelings, with such obvious evidence, so firm, so unavoidable, may be of a coded nature. How can I not know whether I am in love, angry, terrified, or melancholy?

- "The sphere of feeling is continuous and exists at several levels. Life is a constant dialogue in which every moment brings new data of affectivity."[15]

Although it may be difficult to act on the basis of affectivity, inasmuch as we are dealing with life itself in its most fundamental reactions, educators must attempt to *decipher* that intimate dimension of the student, need it, and teach the person how to deal with it in a positive and intelligent way. The lead agent here is a kind of affective intelligence that seeks to develop emotional competence.

In this regard, Marina states that the first criterion of the life of feeling is this: "The human being needs to live with feel-

---

15. Ibid., 26-33.

ings, but also above them. He aspires to live according to well thought-out values; but the tension between values analyzed and values felt produces painful headaches and heartaches."[16]

2.2. Development and education of affectivity in adolescence

2.2.1. PRIMARY EMOTIONALITY AND THE AFFECTIVE CRISIS.

During puberty or early adolescence the influence of affectivity over the psyche increases considerably. There is an intense affective life.

In principle, the vitality and energy proper to this stage favor the tendency to become enthusiastic about almost everything. They also foster passionate behavior. Manifestations of this are, for example, exaggerated and showy responses (shouts, insults, etc.) and angry reactions (for example, an outburst of rage followed by slamming the door).

The affective life of the early teenager is initially characterized by *primary emotional responses*. These are reactions of concern, anger, fear, bitterness, etc. They are affective behaviors involving limited awareness—superficial, spontaneous, based simply on sensible knowledge and desire. They do not reach the level of sentiments, which originate in intellectual knowledge and desire.

This primary affectivity (elementary, not evolved) is made up of isolated emotions, without any control. The pubescent youth abandons himself to emotion and becomes its victim. There is emotional imbalance, which is why the pubescent goes berserk over any trifle, is so unstable and suspicious, has frequent changes of mood and humor.

Primary affectivity is aroused by the typical tensions of this age. Physical changes related to growth and sexual maturation can provoke strong emotional impulses and hyperemotional

16. Ibid., 234.

states; conflicts arising from the pursuit of independence often occasion emotional discharges and aggressive behavior. But the reactions of the teen are not always outwardly directed. When an obstacle prevents him from reaching the goals he has in mind (goals related to autonomy, for example, along with physical appearance, success in school, friendships, participation in the family) he feels frustrated. He does not yet have the capacity to tolerate frustration and to accept contradiction. Thus he feels insecure and under-appreciated. His ego may be so weak that, instead of rebelling, he withdraws into himself. In this way he may become melancholy and depressed. Another way of evading oppressive reality is daydreaming: taking refuge in a world of fantasy created by himself to his own taste.

Withdrawal can lead to guilt feelings, shame, sadness, etc. They show an evolution in affectivity. The teenager is no longer moved by primary emotions; now he needs acceptance, understanding, esteem, love. He needs affection and suffers from any lack of it in his family or circle of friends.

2.2.2. EDUCATIONAL RESPONSES TO THE CHALLENGES
        OF AFFECTIVITY AT PUBERTY

One of the most important challenges to parents and teachers of children during puberty is *to understand them.* A typical complaint of parents at this time is "Nobody can understand this child!" A typical complaint of the children is "My parents don't understand me!" It is a clear symptom of mutual incomprehension when unanswered questions accumulate. Why is she spending so much time in front of the mirror? Why does he have such sudden and changing reactions? Why does he isolate himself? Why doesn't he talk about himself? Why is he always away from home? Why does she avoid her parents?

A second challenge is *to accept him as he is:* impatient, unpredictable, easily angered, shy, disorderly, etc. Nostalgia for the good behavior of childhood is no help. Nor should the child be compared with a responsible adult. That would make him feel guilty, increase the frustrations typical of the age and lead him to attack others and defend himself. All this does is create continual conflicts and tensions in the family and at school. Accepting the child is indispensable so that he, in time, will accept himself.

A third challenge is *knowing how to deal with him*. How should one deal with a teenager to get some improvement in his behavior and not have one's relationship with him deteriorate?

The approach must be loving—for, as we saw earlier, the child is having a hard time and needs to feel loved. If, for example, he has just let us down in some way, instead of exploding it is better that we speak from affection: "This has hurt me; you have failed me again; I did not expect it from you."

To get the child to do what we want, it is more effective to appeal to self-esteem than punishment. Not, "if you don't do it, you will be punished," but, "I ask you this because I trust you; I know you can do it."

This way of acting is not simply a matter of technique. It requires, above all, certain attitudes on the part of parents and teachers. Among these, I would emphasize:

1) Be calm: don't lose your serenity; don't dramatize or be carried away by hurt feelings. Nervous educators share their nervousness with the teenager and damage their relationship. They cause a tempest in a teapot.

2) Try to see new kinds of behavior objectively: as manifestations of evolving development, not as moral defects. Maintain some distance from problems; avoid getting emotionally involved.

3) Learn to listen (it is not enough to look as if one were listening).

4) Take the student or child of this age seriously. Become truly interested in what concerns him. Show him that he is valued and appreciated.

5) Be patient and persevering: do not lose confidence due to a lack of results; start anew each day; know how to wait.

6) Get used to the constant changes of physical and mental growth and to the new reactions they provoke in the child. The child or student is a changing reality, and educators must "accompany" him in this process, willing to make their own adjustments to new situations. This requires great flexibility.

7) Adapt your approach according to sex, character, age, and the aptitudes and interests of individuals. This is advisable at all stages of development, but especially during puberty, since this is the time when personal differences become more pronounced.

8) Be detached from the child or student. One must accept generously and with a sporting spirit the progressive distancing that occurs from parents and teachers in favor of peers and friends. This is the time to correct exaggerated attachments.

A fourth challenge is *to create an environment that will favor the adaptation of the pubescent child to himself and to the reality he is experiencing.* A warm family and school environment, filled with trust, understanding, and affection, will help overcome the fears, sense of shame, false guilt, complexes, feelings of anguish, etc., arising from physical changes during this stage of development.

In such an environment, it is useful for the child to have frequent opportunities of making a good impression on his parents, for as we have seen, that is an important way to improve his self-image and self-esteem. Occasions must be provided for him to do things he is good at. For example, a son with mechanical inclinations might be asked to take care of the family car.

2.3. Affectivity in adolescence

As a consequence of the deepening in intimacy that takes place at this stage, an enrichment of affectivity takes place. All behavior acquires in this way an affective tonality. We witness at this time an interior growth underlying affective behavior.

To understand this phenomenon better it is useful to compare affectivity in middle adolescence to affectivity at earlier stages. The affectivity of the child and the pubescent adolescence is spontaneous, expressive, close to the surface. But that of adolescents above the age of 14 is deeper and secretive. It is much easier to know a child's feelings before or during puberty than in mid-adolescence. In this latter stage he is able to hide his affectivity, and he does; he opens his heart only to an intimate friend.

What is the explanation of this change in affective conduct? Affectivity has become more conscious than before. At an earlier age, each stimulus was followed by an immediate and therefore primary response. In contrast, now there is a moment of reflection between stimulus and response that allows the subject to control the reaction, and to reason about it.

With the interiorization of affective conduct, there is an increase in the practice of withdrawal that began at puberty. The insecurity created by interior changes and new frustrations press the adolescent to hide within himself. In that interior refuge, guilt feelings are generated, together with shame, confusion, discouragement, sadness, anxiety, melancholy, etc.

We are at *the stage of sentiments*. Feelings are the true psychological riches of adolescents. They influence the whole personality, for good or evil. Positive sentiments reinforce and enrich motives and behavior, while negative ones are self-destructive (they can be the origin of poor adaptation and mental disease). What kind of sentiments have a larger role at this time? Among the positive ones are affection, tenderness, joy, friendship, love. Also, those of an artistic, moral, or religious nature. The negative ones are mainly those mentioned above in relation to the behavior of withdrawal.

During middle adolescence *emotional difficulties* may appear, tied to the unfulfilled needs of the personality. Let us see some of these.

1) *Need for identity.* Adolescence is an evolving phase in which one seeks personal identity (to be somebody— myself, the one I want and ought to be). But the adolescent does not always find an identity easily. During this long search, the adolescent feels uncertainty about who he is, his future roles, his capacity to assume future responsibility. At times the uncertainty turns into anxiety.

2) *Need for affection.* The adolescent feels habitually insecure, misunderstood, attacked, humiliated, guilty, alone. He needs a lot of affection and emotional support. Without these, he can fall into anxiety.

3) *Need for personal realization.* The adolescent feels a need to grow as much on the outside as inside. Progressively more autonomous behavior places him in situations of success or failure. Success feeds a positive self-concept and heightens self-esteem; failure produces discouragement, low personal esteem, guilt, all of which also predisposes one to anxiety. A typical example is that of the student who had never before failed a subject but early in college fails several. Unexpected failure upsets him and leads him to think he is no good and should drop out.

4) *Need for independence.* The adolescent needs the following: some freedom of coming and going in his way

of living; the ability to make at least some personal decisions; the ability to act in pursuit of his legitimate interests; the ability to have his own things, and also to preserve his inner world from snoopers. When family or school norms fail to respect all of these needs, aggressive, rebellious, or inappropriate behavior is likely to result.

5) *Need of social relationships.* The adolescent needs a harmonious relationship with his classmates and companions, close friends, parents, and professors. Without it, he will frequently fall into resentment, melancholy, and aggression. (Especially so when the problem is due to his own incapacity to relate.)

2.4. The challenge of children's friendships

Parents take second place to friends during adolescence. Parents worry about the influence of possibly bad friends; they may even become jealous of their children's friends. All this may lead them to intervene in the choice of friends; to forbid friendships; to raise obstacles to their children's relationships with their friends.

These are attitudes to avoid. They are not only unjust and disrespectful but create conflicts with children. And they reveal a deeper problem: some parents do not value friendship; they are not aware of the role of friendships in the formation of the personality of their adolescent child. Another deep-seated problem is to love children possessively, with a love that seeks to exclude potential rivals. Parents must let their children freely choose their friends because freedom is essential to friendship. (It can, however, coexist with educational guidance in regard to friendships.)

Parents must not only accept but encourage the friendships of their children (for example, making it easy for the friends to come to their home). It is highly desirable that they know how to detach themselves progressively from their children, something essential if the children are to exercise their freedom and learn to make their own decisions.

2.5. *Problems associated with the education of affectivity*

The following problems appear mainly during adolescence:

1) Reactive responses not appropriate to rational and voluntary behavior. Responses may be out of proportion to the stimuli.
2) Contradictory feelings.
3) Behavior dominated by excessive emotion.
4) Incapacity to control and direct feelings. Overflowing affectivity.
5) An affective life shaped by desires or impulses and not controlled by the will. Rationalization of desires: reasons are invented to justify desires.
6) The feelings of the moment become the criteria for decisions.

2.6. *Basic goals of the education of affectivity*

1) Self-control and self-government of the feelings by the will. The following may be helpful: avoiding situations of conflict (by taking a detour, for example); engaging in sports (reducing the emotional level); fulfilling the duty of the moment; laughter (which produces an emotional discharge); thinking positively about others; having a good sense of humor (which allows a person to see things in the best light).
2) Acquiring the habit of reflection (this makes it difficult for feelings to be directed by desire).
3) Encouraging feelings that are elevated and positive, good sentiments (joy, enthusiasm, tenderness, compassion, etc.).

4) Cultivating delicacy in feelings.

5) Learning to recognize one's own feelings and those of others.

6) Learning to express feelings.

7) Learning how to suffer (that is, learning to love).

8) Learning how to evaluate one's own feelings. Marina proposes three criteria. First, feelings that impede freedom are bad; second, feelings that encourage good behavior are good; third, feelings about a particular value may or may not be appropriate.[17]

9) Learning to be emotionally intelligent.

Emotional intelligence is a form of practical intelligence that combines thoughts and emotions. It is a capacity that allows one to harmonize heart and mind, especially in difficult moments. It involves raising to a conscious level those aspects of emotional life that had been hidden, so that, instead of being an obstacle, they can be a help to successful work and relationships with others. Emotional intelligence, then, is the intelligent use of emotions, based on the ability to discern one's own feelings and those of others.

The intelligent use of emotions has two aspects. The first consists of controlling them by addressing their causes. It involves mastering negative feelings such as insecurity, anxiety, irritability, anger, etc. It also includes learning to reject complications and dramatization, not attributing bad intentions to others, etc. If all this is not accomplished, performance will suffer and conflicts will increase, not only in the family but at work.

The second aspect consists in utilizing emotions in a positive way and drawing advantages from some of them. In this

---

17. Ibid., 230-241.

way, they become factors of motivation, of good communication with others, etc. Some types of emotional control concern one's relationship with oneself: self-consciousness, self-control, self-motivation, etc. These characteristics are seen in those who can accept their problems and draw strength from their weaknesses, etc. Other abilities pertain to relationships with others: empathy, social wisdom (persuasion, communication, leadership, team work, solving conflicts, etc.). They are proper to those who communicate well with others, harmonize readily with people, make friends easily anywhere, etc.[18]

---

18. G. Castillo, *Anatomía de una historia de amor* (Pamplona: EUNSA, 2002): 217-220.

Bibliography*

Alonso García, J. and Román Sánchez, J. M. *Educación familiar y autoconcepto en niños pequeños*. Madrid: Pirámide, 2003.

Altarejos, F., Martínez, M., Buxarrais, M. R., and Bernal, A. *Familia, valores y educación*, XXIII Seminario Interuniversitario de Teoría de la Educación, Santiago (2004). (*HTTP://aula.cesga.es/SITE04/document/Ponencias/ponencia_2.pdf*)

Altarejos, F., Naval, C., and González-Simancas, J. L. "La confianza: exigencia de la libertad personal," in A. Malo, ed., *La dignita della persona humana*. Rome: Edizioni Università della Santa Croce, 2003: 229–242.

Altarejos, F. and Rodríguez, A. "Identidad, coexistencia y familia," *Estudios sobre educación*, 6 (2004): 105–118.

Altarejos, F., Rodríguez, A., Bernal, A. "*La familia, forja de la sociabilidad: aceptación y donación*." II Congreso Internacional de la Familia, *La familia, el futuro de la sociedad*, Palma de Mallorcia, 22–24 de noviembre, 2004.

Altarejos, F., Rodríguez, A., and Fontrodona, J. *Retos educativos de la globalización. Hacia una sociedad solidaria*. Pamplona: EUNSA, 2003.

Amato, P. R. and Booth, A. *A Generation at Risk: Growing Up in an Era of Family Upheaval*. Cambridge, MA: Harvard University, 1997.

---

* The original reference has been copied, followed, when possible, by the English version. The pages do not correspond. Most of them are available through Amazon.

Amato, P. R. and Deboer, D. "The Transmission of Marital Instability Across Generations: Relationship Skills or Commitment to Marriage?" *Journal of Marriage and Family*, 63 (2001): 1038–1051.

Aquinos, T. *De Veritate, Cuestion 22, El apetito del bien*. Pamplona: Servicio de Publicaciones de la Universidad de Navarra, 2001.

Aron, R. *Las etapas del pensamiento sociológico. Durkheim, Pareto, Weber*. Buenos Aires: Siglo Veinte, 1992. [*Main Currents in Sociological Thought, Vol. II: Durkheim, Pareto Weber*. Garden City, NY: Anchor Books, 1970.]

Audigier, F. *Teaching about Society Passing on Values. Elementary Law in Civic Education. A Secondary Education for Europe*. Strasbourg: Council of Europe Publishing, 1996.

Beck-Gernsheim, E. *La reinvención de la familia: en busca de nuevas formas de convivencia*. Barcelona: Paidós, 2003. [*The Reinvention of the Family: In Search of New Lifestyles*. Cambridge, Oxford, and Boston: Polity, 2002.]

Bernal, A. "Hace diez años: Año Internacional de la Familia," *Estudios sobre Educación*, Pamplona, 6 (2004): 77–88.

Bertalanffy, L. Von. *Perspectivas en la teoría general de sistemas: estudios científico-filosóficos*, Madrid: Alianza, 1979. [*Perspectives on General Systems Theory: Scientific-Philosophical Studies*. New York: George Braziller, 1976.]

Bogenschneider, K. "Has Family Policy Come of Age? A Decade Review of the State of the U.S. Family Policy in the 1990s," in R. M. Milardo, ed., *Understanding Families. Into the New Millenium: A Decade in Review*. Lawrence: NCFR, 2001, 355–378.

Bowlby, J. *La separación*. Buenos Aires: Piados, 1997. [*Separation*. (Vol. 2 of *Attachment and Loss*), London: Hogarth Press, 1973.]

———. *El vínculo afectivo*. Barcelona: Piados, 1997. [*Attachment and Loss*. New York: Basic Books, 1969.]

Bradon, H. "Major Trends Affecting Families Worldwide," in *Family Matters*, 45 (August, 2003). Bulletin of the International Year of the Family. *http://www.un.org/esa/socdev/family/Publications/Family-Matters/(2004March)*.

Buber, M. *Yo y tú*. Madrid: Caparrós, 1993. [*I and thou*. London: Hesperides Press, 2006.]

Buchanan, A. "Assessing Communitarian Critique of Liberalism," *Ethics*, 99 (1989): 852–882.

Buttiglione, R. *La persona y la familia*. Madrid: Palabra, 1999.

Castilla Cortázar, B. *Persona y género: ser varón y ser mujer*. Barcelona: Ediciones Internacionales Universitarias, 1997.

Castillo, G. *El Adolescente y sus retos*. Madrid: Pirámide, 2002. [*Teenagers and Their Problems*. Dublin: Four Court Press Ltd., 1986.]

———. *Anatomía de una historia de amor*. Pamplona: EUNSA, 2002.

Choza, J. *La supresión del pudor*. Pamplona: EUNSA, 1980.

Christenson, S. L. and Sheridan, S. M. *Schools and Families: Creating Essential Connections for Learning*. New York: The Guilford Press, 2001.

Coleman, J. S. "Social Capital in the Creation of Human Capital," *American Journal of Sociology*, 94 (1988), Supplement, S95–S120.

Colomina, R. "Activitat conjunta i influencia educativa en el context familiar," *Educar*, 28 (2001): 181–204.

Coltrane, S. "The Paradox of Fatherhood: Predicting the Future of Men's Family Involvement," in W. D. Allen and L. Eiklenborg, eds., *Vision 2003: Contemporary Family Issues*. Minneapolis: National Council on Family Relations, 2003.

Constable, R. and Lee, D. B. *Social Work with Families: Content and Process*. Chicago: Lyceum Books, 2004.

Coombs, P. H. *La crisis mundial de la educación*. New York: Oxford University Press, 1968. [*The World Educational Crisis: A Systems Analysis*. New York: Oxford University Press, 1968.]

Coontz, S. "Historical Perspectives of Family Studies," in R. M. Milardo, ed., *Understanding Families. Into the New Millenium: A Decade in Review*. Lawrence: NCFR, 2001: 80–94.

Crosnoe, R. "Social Capital and the Interplay of Families and Schools," *Journal of Marriage and Family*, 66 (5), (2004): 267–280.

D'Agostino, F. *Elementos para una filosofía de la familia*. Madrid: Rialp, 1991.

Delgado-Gaitán, C. "School Matters in the Mexican-American Home: Socializing Children to Education," in *American Educational Research Journal*, 29 (3), (1992): 495–513.

Delhors, J., ed. *La educación encierra un tesoro*. Madrid: Santillana-Ediciones, UNESCO, 1996. [*Education Encompasses a Treasure*. UNESCO.]

Demo, D. H. and Cox, M. J. "Families with Young Children: A Review of Research in the 1990s," *Journal of Marriage and Family*, 62 (2000): 876–895.

———. "Families in the Middle and Later Years: A Review and Critique of Research in the 1990s," in R. M. Milardo, ed., *Understanding Families. Into the New Millenium: A Decade in Review*, Lawrence: NCFR, 2001: 95–114.

Digby, A., ed. *Full Circle? Bringing up Children in the Post-Permissivem Society*. Exeter, GB: Crowley Esmonde Ltd., 1988.

Donati, P. *Manual de Sociología de la familia*. Pamplona: EUNSA, 2003.

Durkheim, E. *Educación y sociología*. Barcelona: Península, 1996. [*Education and Sociology*. Glencoe, IL: Free Press, 1956.]

———. *Educación como socialización*. Salamanca: Sígueme, 1976.

———. *L'Education morale*. Paris: Alcan, 1925.

———. *De la division du travail social*, 4th ed. Paris: P.U.F., 1996.

Elzo, J., et al. *Hijos y padres. Comunicación y conflictos*. Madrid: FAD, 2002.

Erdman, P. and Caffery, T. *Attachment and Family Systems*. New York: Brunner-Routledge, 2001.

Esquer, H. *El límite del pensamiento. La propuesta metodológica de Leonardo Polo*. Pamplona: EUNSA, 2000.

Farrell, A., Tayler, C., and Tennent, L. "Building Social Capital in Early Childhood Education and Care: An Australian Study," *British Educational Research Journal*, 30 (5), (2004): 623–633.

Ferrarotti, F. *El pensamiento sociológico: de Augusto Comte a Marx Horkheimer*. Barcelona: Península, 1975.

Frank, R. *The Involved Father: Family-Tested Solutions for Getting Dads to Participate More in the Daily Lives of Their Children*. New York: St. Martin's Press, 1999.

Frankl, V. *El hombre en busca de sentido.* Barcelona: Herder, 1983. [*Man's Search for Meaning.* Boston: Beacon Press, 1959.]

Ganong, L. H. and Coleman, M. "Family Resilience in Multiple Contexts," *Journal of Marriage and Family,* 64 (2002): 346–348.

García Garrido, J. L. *Los fundamentos de la educación social.* Madrid: EMESA, 1971.

García-Hoz, V. *Educación personalizada.* Madrid: Rialp, 1988.

Giddens, A. *Un mundo desbocado. Los efectos de la globalización en nuestras vidas.* Madrid: Taurus, 2000. [*Runaway World: How Globalization is Affecting Our Lives.* London: Profile, 1999.]

Gimeno, A. *La familia: el desafío de la diversidad.* Barcelona: Ariel, 1999.

Glantz, M. D. and Johnson, J. L., eds. *Resilience and Development: Positive Life Adaptations.* New York: Kluwer Academic/Plenum Publishers, 1999.

Goleman, D. *Inteligencia emocional.* Barcelona: Kairós, 1995. [*Emotional Intelligence.* New York: Bantam Books, 1995.]

González-Simancas, J. L. *Educación: libertad y compromiso.* Pamplona: EUNSA, 1992.

Grusec, J. E. and Kuczynski, L. *Parenting and Children's Internationalization of Values: A Handbook of Contemporary Theory.* New York: John Wiley & Sons, 1997.

Guardini, R. *Virtù.* Brescia: Morcelliana, 1997. [*Learning the Virtues.* Manchester, NH: Sophia Institute Press, 2000.]

Harris, K. M., Furstenberg, F. and Marmer, J. "Parental Involvement with Adolescents in Intact Families: The Influence of Fathers over the Life Course." *Demography,* 35 (1998): 201–216.

Hervada, J. *Diálogos sobre el amor y el matrimonio.* Pamplona: EUNSA, 1987.

Hetherington, E. M. and Kelly, J. *For Better or For Worse: Divorce Reconsidered.* New York: W.W. Norton & Company, Inc., 2002.

Holmes, S. *The Anatomy of Antiliberalism.* Cambridge, MA: Harvard University Press, 1993.

I.N.E., *Cifras,* 15 May, 2004; *http://www.ine.es/revistas/cifraine/ cifine_15mayo.pdf.*

Jacobvitz, D. "Fostering Resilience in Children: The Importance of Early Relationship Experiences," in W. D. Allen and L. Eiklenborg, eds., *Vision 2003: Contemporary Family Issues*, Minneapolis: National Council on Family Relations, 2003: 53–58.

Jenkins, C., McHale, S. and Crouter, A. "Dimensions of Mothers and Fathers—Differential Treatment of Siblings: Links with Adolescents' Sex-Typed Personal Qualities," *Family Relations*, 52 (2002): 82–89.

Johnson, P. *Tiempos modernos*. Buenos Aires: Javier Vergara, ed., 1988. [*Modern Times Revised Edition: The World from the Twenties to the Nineties*. New York: Perennial Classics, 1991.]

John Paul II. *Familiaris Consortio*. 2000.

Kant, I. *Fundamentación de la metafísica de las costumbres*. Barcelona: Ariel, 1996. [*Fundamental Principles of the Metaphysics of Morals*. Paperback, 2007.]

Kottak, C. P. *Espejo para la humanidad. Introducción a la Antropología cultural*. Madrid: McGraw-Hill, 3rd ed., 2003. [*Cultural Anthropology*. McGraw-Hill, 2003.]

Leon, K. "Risk and Protective Factors in Young Children's Adjustment to Parental Divorce: A Review of the Research," *Family Relations*, 52 (2003): 258–270.

Lewis, C. S. *The Weight of Glory*. New York: HaperCollins, 2001.

López Quintás, A. *El secreto de una vida lograda: curso de pedagogía del amor y la familia*. Madrid: Palabra, 2003.

Llano, C. *Las formas actuales de la libertad*. México City: Trillas, 1983.

MacIntyre, A. *Animales racionales y dependientes. Por qué los seres humanos necesitamos las virtudes*. Barcelona: Paidós, 2001. [*Dependent Rational Animals: Why Human Beings Need the Virtues*. Chicago: Open Court Books, 1999.]

Mallet, S. "Understanding Home: A Critical Review of the Literature," *The Sociological Review*, 52 (1), (2004): 62–89.

Marañón, G. *Tiberio. Historia de un Resentido*. Madrid: Espasa-Calpe, 1981. [*Tiberius: The Resentful Caesar*. New York: Duell, Sloan and Pearce, 1956.]

Marías, J. *Mapa del mundo personal*. Madrid: Alianza Editorial, 1994.

Marina, J. A. *El laberinto sentimental*. Barcelona: Anagrama, 1996.

Markman, H. J., Stanley, S. M., and Kline, G. H. "Why Marriage Education Can Work and How Government Can Be Involved: Illustrations from the PREP (the Prevention and Relationship Enhancement Program) Approach," in WQ. D. Allen, and L. Eiklenborg, eds., *Vision 2003: Contemporary Family Issues*. Minneapolis: National Coucil on Family Relations, 2003: 16–26.

Martín López, E. *Familia y sociedad. Una introducción a la sociología de la familia*. Madrid: Rialp, 2000.

Méda, D. *El tiempo de las mujeres. Conciliación entre vida familiar y profesional entre hombres y mujeres*. Madrid: Narcera, 2002.

Milardo, R. M. "Preface. The Decade in Review," in *Understanding Families. Into the New Millenium: A Decade in Review*. Lawrence: NCFR, 2001: vii–ix.

Millán-Puelles, A. *Sobre el hombre y la sociedad*. Madrid: Rialp, 1976.

———. *La formación de la personalidad humana*. Madrid: Rialp, 1963.

Morin, E. *Introducción al pensamiento complejo*. Barcelona: Gedisa, 1997.

Myers-Walls, J. A. and Somlai, P., eds. *Families as Educators for Global Citizenship*. Ashgate, VT., 2001.

Múgica, F. *Emile Durkheim. Civilización y división del trabajo (II). La naturaleza moral del vínculo social*. Pamplona: Cuaderno Anuario Filosófico, n. 12, 2004.

Naval, C. *Educar ciudadanos*. Pamplona: EUNSA, 1995.

———. *Educar ciudadanos, La polémica liberal-communitarista en educación*, 2nd edition. Pamplona: EUNSA, 2000.

Neira, T. "*Pedagogía y educación familiar*," in Castillo, E., ed. *Educación familiar: nuevas relaciones humanas y humanizadoras*. Madrid: Narcea, 2002.

Newman, J. H. *Persuadido por la Verdad*. Madrid: Encuentro, 1995.

Otero, F. *La libertad en la familia*. Pamplona: EUNSA, 1982.

Palacios, M. J. *Familia y desarrollo humano*. Madrid: Alianza, 1989: 39.

Parkin, R. and Stone, L. *Kinship and Family: An Anthropological Reader.* London: Blackwell, 2004.

Parsons, T. and Bales, R. F. *Family Socialization and Interaction Process.* New York: Free Press, 1955.

Pérez Alonso-Geta, P., ed. *Valores y pautas de interacción familiar en la adolescencia (13–18 años).* Madrid: Fundación Santa María, 2002.

Pieper, J. *Amor,* in *Las virtudes fundamentales.* Madrid: Rialp, 1997.

Polaino, A. *Familia y autoestima.* Barcelona: Ariel, 2003.

Polo, L. *Ética. Hacia una versión moderna de los temas clásicos.* Madrid: Unión Editorial, 1996.

————. *Sobre la existencia cristiana.* Pamplona: EUNSA, 1996.

————. *La persona humana y su crecimiento.* Pamplona: EUNSA, 1996.

————. *Quien es el hombre: un espíritu en el tiempo,* 5th ed. Madrid: Rialp, 2003.

————. *Antropología Trascendental I.* Pamplona: EUNSA, 1999.

Powell, L. H. *Family Life Education: An Introduction.* Mountainview, CA: Mayfield, 2001.

Pruett, K. D. *Fatherneed: Why Father Care Is as Essential as Mother Care for Your Child.* New York: Free Press, 2000.

Rodrigo, M. J., and Palacios, J., eds. *Familia y desarrollo humano.* Madrid: Alianza, 1998.

Rodríguez, A., Parra, C., and Altarejos, F. *Pensar la sociedad. Una iniciación a la sociología,* 2nd ed. Pamplona: EUNSA, 2003.

Sahay, A. *Max Weber y la sociología moderna.* Buenos Aires: Paidos, 1974.

Sandel, M. J. *Liberalism and its critics.* Oxford: Basil Blackwell, 1984.

Sanguineti, J. J. *Lógica,* 5th ed. Pamplona: EUNSA, 2000.

Séneca. *Epístolas morales a Lucilio, I (Libros I–IX; Epístolas I–80).* Madrid: Gredos, 1986.

Scheler, M. *El resentimiento en la moral.* Madrid: Caparrós Editores, 1993. [*Ressentiment.* Glencoe, IL: Free Press, 1959.]

Skolnick, S. "Uncle Sam, Matchmaker: Marriage as a Public Policy," in W. D. Allen and L. Eiklenborg, eds., *Vision 2003: Contemporary*

Family Issues. Minneapolis: National Council on Family Relations, 2003: 11–15.

Spaemann, R. *Personas. Acerca de la distinción entre algo y alguien.* Pamplona: EUNSA, 2000. [*Persons: The Difference between "Someone" and "Something."* Oxford Studies in Theological Ethics: Oxford University Press, 2007.]

Stone, L. *Kinship and Family: An Anthropological Reader.* London: Blackwell, 2004.

Suares, M. *Mediando en sistemas familiares.* Barcelona: Paidos, 2002.

Tiryakian, E. *Sociologismo y existencialismo. Dos enfoques sobre el individuo y la sociedad.* Buenos Aires: Amorrortu Editores, 1962.

Turner, R. *Family Interaction.* New York: John Wiley & Sons, 1970.

Tönnies, F. *Community and Association.* London: Routledge & Kegan Paul, 1974.

UN General Assembly. Preparation for the Tenth Anniversary of the International Year of the Family in 2004. No 57/139, 17 July 2002 (A/57/139).

UN Department of Economic and Social Affairs. Preparation for the Tenth Anniversary of the International Year of the Family in 2004. Report of the Secretary General. 41 Session, 10–21 February, 2003 (E/CN.5/2003/6).

UN Department of Economic and Social Affairs. Session Dec. 10–12, 2003, in *http://www.un.org/esa/socdev/family.*

Ugarte, F. *Del resentimiento al perdón. Una puerta a la felicidad.* Madrid: Rialp, 2004. [*From Resentment to Forgiveness: A Gateway to Happiness.* New York: Scepter Publishers, 2008.]

Vildarich, J. L. *El ser conyugal.* Madrid: Rialp, 2001.

———. *El modelo antropológico del matrimonio.* Madrid: Rialp, 2001.

Walberg, H. J. "Improving the Productivity of America's Schools," *Educational Leadership*, 41 (8), (1984): 19–27.

——— and Lai, J. "Meta-analytic Effects of Policy," in G. J. Cizek, ed., *Handbook of Educational Policy*, San Diego, CA: Academic, 1999: 418–454.

Walker, J. "Radiating Messages: An International Perspective," *Family Relations*, 52 (2003): 406–417.

Walker, S., and Riley, D. "Involvement of the Personal Social Network as a Factor in Parent Education Effectiveness," *Family Relations*, 50, (2), (2001): 186–193.

Wang, M. C., Haertl, G. D. and Walberg, H. J. *Building Educational Resilience.* Bloomington, IN: Phi Delta Kappan Educational Foundation, 1998.

Weber, M. *Economía y Sociedad. Esbozo de una sociología comprensiva.* México: Fondo de Cultura Económica, 1984. [*Economy and Society: An Outline of Interpretive Sociology.* New York: Routledge, 1979.]

————. *Essais sur la théorie de la science, traduit de l'allemand et introduit par Julien Freund.* Paris: Plon, 1965.

————. *Ensayos sobre la metodología sociológica.* Buenos Aires: Amorrortu, 1982.

Wiley, A. R., and Ebata, A. "Reaching American Families: Making Diversity Real in Family Life Education," *Family Relations*, 53 (2004): 273–281.

Wojtyla, K. *El hombre y su destino. Ensayos de Antropología.* Madrid: Rialp, 1998.

Zubiri, X. *Cinco lecciones de filsofía.* Madrid: Alianza Editorial, 2002.

Index